CAMBRIDGE LIBRARY COLLECTION

Books of enduring scholarly value

Education

This series focuses on educational theory and practice, particularly in the context of eighteenth- and nineteenth-century Europe and its colonies, and America. During this period, the questions of who should be educated, to what age, to what standard and using what curriculum, were widely debated. The reform of schools and universities, the drive towards improving women's education, and the movement for free (or at least low-cost) schools for the poor were all major concerns both for governments and for society at large. The books selected for reissue in this series discuss key issues of their time, including the 'appropriate' levels of instruction for the children of the working classes, the emergence of adult education movements, and proposals for the higher education of women. They also cover topics that still resonate today, such as the nature of education, the role of universities in the diffusion of knowledge, and the involvement of religious groups in establishing and running schools.

Letters on the Improvement of the Mind

Originally published in 1773 in two volumes, and now reissued here together in one, this work by the writer Hester Chapone (1727–1801), a renowned proponent of female education, contains advice delivered in the form of letters to her niece. The first volume deals primarily with matters of religion and morality, while the second volume addresses questions of behaviour and schooling. Unusually for self-improvement books of this era, Chapone recommends that a young woman should have a rigorous education in a wide variety of subjects, including ancient history and geography, as well as instruction in ladylike deportment and mastery of household matters. She exhorts young ladies to avoid vanity and other vices through devoted study of scripture, and writes of the importance of choosing worthy and sensible friends who can be trusted to offer good advice. Chapone's posthumously published works, in two volumes, are also reissued in this series.

T0381840

Cambridge University Press has long been a pioneer in the reissuing of out-of-print titles from its own backlist, producing digital reprints of books that are still sought after by scholars and students but could not be reprinted economically using traditional technology. The Cambridge Library Collection extends this activity to a wider range of books which are still of importance to researchers and professionals, either for the source material they contain, or as landmarks in the history of their academic discipline.

Drawing from the world-renowned collections in the Cambridge University Library and other partner libraries, and guided by the advice of experts in each subject area, Cambridge University Press is using state-of-the-art scanning machines in its own Printing House to capture the content of each book selected for inclusion. The files are processed to give a consistently clear, crisp image, and the books finished to the high quality standard for which the Press is recognised around the world. The latest print-on-demand technology ensures that the books will remain available indefinitely, and that orders for single or multiple copies can quickly be supplied.

The Cambridge Library Collection brings back to life books of enduring scholarly value (including out-of-copyright works originally issued by other publishers) across a wide range of disciplines in the humanities and social sciences and in science and technology.

Letters on the Improvement of the Mind

Addressed to a Young Lady

HESTER CHAPONE

CAMBRIDGE
UNIVERSITY PRESS

CAMBRIDGE
UNIVERSITY PRESS

University Printing House, Cambridge, CB2 8BS, United Kingdom

Published in the United States of America by Cambridge University Press, New York

Cambridge University Press is part of the University of Cambridge.
It furthers the University's mission by disseminating knowledge in the pursuit of
education, learning and research at the highest international levels of excellence.

www.cambridge.org
Information on this title: www.cambridge.org/9781108067973

© in this compilation Cambridge University Press 2014

This edition first published 1773
This digitally printed version 2014

ISBN 978-1-108-06797-3 Paperback

LETTERS

ON THE

IMPROVEMENT

OF THE

MIND.

ADDRESSED TO A YOUNG LADY.

I CONSIDER AN HUMAN SOUL WITHOUT EDU-
CATION, LIKE MARBLE IN THE QUARRY,
WHICH SHEWS NONE OF ITS INHERENT
BEAUTIES TILL THE SKILL OF THE POLISHER
FETCHES OUT THE COLOURS, MAKES THE
SURFACE SHINE, AND DISCOVERS EVERY
ORNAMENTAL CLOUD, SPOT AND VEIN THAT
RUNS THRO' THE BODY OF IT. EDUCATION,
AFTER THE SAME MANNER, WHEN IT WORKS
UPON A NOBLE MIND, DRAWS OUT TO VIEW
EVERY LATENT VIRTUE AND PERFECTION,
WHICH WITHOUT SUCH HELPS ARE NEVER
ABLE TO MAKE THEIR APPEARANCE.
ADDISON.

IN TWO VOLUMES.

DUBLIN:
Printed for J. Exshaw, H. Saunders, W.
Sleater, J. Potts, D. Chamberlaine,
J. Williams, and R. Moncrieffe.
MDCCLXXIII.

T O

Mrs. MONTAGU.

MADAM,

I Believe, you are perfuaded
that I never entertained a
thought of appearing in public,
when the defire of being ufeful
to one dear child, in whom I
take the tendereft intereft, in-
duced me to write the following
Letters: — perhaps it was the
partiality of friendfhip, which

fo far biaffed your judgment, as
to make you think them capable
of being more extenfively ufeful,
and warmly to recommend the
publication of them. — Though
this partiality could alone prevent
your judgment from being confidered as decifive in favour of the
work it is more flattering to the
writer than any literary fame;
if, however, you will allow me
to add, that fome ftrokes of
your elegant pen have corrected
thefe Letters, I may hope, they
will be received with an attention,
which

which will enfure a candid judgement from the reader, and perhaps
will enable them to make fome ufeful impreffions on thofe, to whom
they are now particularly offered.

They only, who know how
your hours are employed, and of
what important value they are to
the good and happinefs of individuals, as well as to the delight and
improvement of the public, can
juftly eftimate my obligation to you
for the time and confideration you
have beftowed on this little work.—
As *you* have drawn it forth, I may

claim

claim a fort of right to the ornament and protection of your name,
and to the privilege of publicly pro-
feſſing myſelf, with the higheſt
eſteem,

MADAM,

your much obliged friend,

and moſt obedient

humble ſervant,

THE AUTHOR.

CONTENTS.

V O L. II.

L E T.

L E T T E R I.

MY DEAREST NIECE,

THOUGH you are fo happy as to
have parents, who are both capable and defirous of giving you all
proper inftruction, yet I, who love you
fo tenderly, cannot help fondly wifhing to
contribute fomething, if poffible, to your
improvement and welfare :—And, as I
am fo far feparated from you, that it is
only by pen and ink I can offer you my
fentiments, I will hope that your attention
may be engaged, by feeing on paper,
from the hand of one of your warmeft
friends, Truths of the higheft importance,
which, though you may not find new,
can never be too deeply engraven on
your mind. Some of them perhaps, may
make no great impreffion at prefent,
and yet may fo far gain a place in your

A   me-

memory, as readily to return to your
thoughts when occaſion recalls them.—
And, if you pay me the compliment of
preſerving my letters, you may poſſibly
re-peruſe them at ſome future period,
when concurring circumſtances may give
them additional weight ;—and thus they
may prove more effectual than the ſame
things ſpoken in converſation. — But,
however this may prove, I cannot reſiſt
the deſire of trying to be in ſome degree uſeful to you, on your ſetting out
in a life of trial and difficulty ; your
ſucceſs in which, muſt determine your
fate for ever.

Hitherto you have " thought as a child,
" and underſtood as a child ; but it is
" time to put away childiſh things."—
You are now in your fifteenth year, and
muſt ſoon act for yourſelf ; therefore it
is high time to ſtore your mind with thoſe
principles, which muſt direct your conduct, and fix your character. — If you
deſire to live in peace and honour, in
favour with God and man, and to die
in the glorious hope of riſing from the

grave

grave to a life of endlefs happinefs—if
thefe things appear worthy of your ambition, you muft fet out in earneft in the
purfuit of them,—Virtue and happinefs
are not attained by, chance, nor by a
cold and languid approbation ; they muft
be fought with ardour, attended to with
diligence, and every affiftance muft be
eagerly embraced, that may enable you
to obtain them.—Confider, that good and
evil are now before you ;—that, if you do
not heartily choofe and love the one, you
muft undoubtedly be the wretched victim
of the other.—Your trial is now begun—
you muft either become one of the glorious *children* of *God*, who are to rejoice
in his love for ever, or a *child* of *deftruction*
—miferable in this life, and punifhed with
eternal death hereafter.—Surely, you will
be impreffed by fo awful a fituation ! you
will earneftly pray to be directed into that
road of life, which leads to excellence and
happinefs—and, you will be thankful to
every kind hand that is held out, to fet
you forward in your journey.

The

The firſt ſtep muſt be to awaken your mind to a ſenſe of the importance of the taſk before you; which is no leſs than to bring your frail nature to that degree of Chriſtian perfection, which is to qualify it for immortality, and, without which, it is neceſſarily incapable of happineſs; for, it is a truth never to be forgotten, that God has annexed happineſs to virtue, and miſery to vice, by the unchangeable nature of things; and that, a wicked being (while he continues ſuch) is in a natural incapacity of enjoying happineſs, even with the concurrence of all thoſe outward circumſtances, which in a virtuous mind would produce it.

As there are degrees of virtue and vice, ſo are there of reward and puniſhment, both here and hereafter: But, do not, my deareſt Niece, aim only at eſcaping the dreadful doom of the wicked;— let your deſires take a nobler flight, and aſpire after thoſe tranſcendent honours, and that brighter crown of glory, which await thoſe. who have excelled in virtue —and, let the animating thought, that
every

every fecret effort to gain his favour is noted by your all-feeing Judge, and that he will, with infinite goodnefs, proportion your reward to your labours, excite every faculty of your foul to pleafe and ferve him.—To this end, you muft *inform your underftanding* what you ought to *believe*, and to *do*.—You muft *correct* and *purify* your *heart*; cherifh and improve all its good affections; and continually mortify and fubdue thofe that are evil.—You muft *form* and *govern* your *temper* and *manners*, according to the laws of benevolence and juftice; and qualify yourfelf, by all means in your power, for an *ufeful* and *agreeable* member of fociety.—All this you fee is no light bufinefs, nor can it be performed without a fincere and earneft application of the mind, as to its great and conftant object. —When once you confider life, and the duties of life, in this manner, you will liften eagerly to the voice of inftruction and admonition; and feize every opportunity of improvement; every ufeful hint will be laid up in your heart, and your

A 3   chief

chief delight will be in thoſe perſons, and thoſe books, from which you can learn true wiſdom.

The only ſure foundation of human virtue is religion, and the foundation and firſt principle of religion is the belief of the one only God, and a juſt ſenſe of his attributes.—This you will think you have learn'd long ſince, and poſſeſs in common with almoſt every human creature in this enlightened age and nation ; but, believe me, it is leſs common than you imagine, to believe in the true God — that is, to form ſuch a notion of the Deity as is agreeable to truth, and conſiſtent with thoſe infinite perfections, which all profeſs to aſcribe to him. To form worthy notions of the ſupreme Being, as far as we are capable, is eſſential to true religion and morality ; for as it is our duty to imitate thoſe qualities of the Divinty, which are imitable by us, ſo it is neceſſary we ſhould know what they are, and fatal to miſtake them.—Can thoſe who think of God with ſervile dread and terror, as of a

gloomy

gloomy tyrant, armed with almighty
power to torment and deſtroy them, be
ſaid to believe in the true God ?—in that
God who, the Scriptures ſay, is love ?—
The kindeſt and beſt of Beings, who
made all creatures in bountiful goodneſs,
that he might communicate to them ſome
portion of his own unalterable happineſs !
—who condeſcends to ſtile himſelf our
Father—and, who pitieth us, as a father
pitieth his own children! Can thoſe who
expect to pleaſe God by cruelty to themſelves, or to their fellow-creatures — by
horrid puniſhments of their own bodies
for the ſin of their ſouls — or, by more
horrid perſecution of others for difference
of opinion, be called true believers ? Have
they not ſet up another God in their
own minds, who rather reſembles the
worſt of beings than the beſt ?—Nor do
thoſe act on ſurer principles who think to
gain the favour of God by ſenſeleſs en-
thuſiaſm and frantic raptures, more like
the wild exceſſes of the moſt depraved
human love, than that reaſonable adoration, that holy reverential love, which is

due

due to the pure and holy Father of the universe.—Those likewise, who murmur against his providence and repine under the restraint of his commands, cannot firmly believe him infinitely wise and good.—If we are not disposed to trust him for future events, to banish fruitless anxiety, and to believe that all things work together for good to those that love him, surely we do not really believe in the God of mercy and truth.—If we wish to avoid all remembrance of him, all communion with him, as much as we dare, surely we do not believe him to be the source of joy and comfort, the dispenser of all good.

How lamentable is it, that so few hearts should feel the pleasures of real piety !— that prayer and thankfgiving should be performed, as they too often are, not with joy, and love, and gratitude ; but, with cold indifference, melancholy dejection, or secret horror !—it is true, we are all such frail and sinful creatures, that we justly fear to have offended our gracious Father ; but, let us remember the

con-

condition of his forgivenefs; If you have
finned—"fin no more."—He is ready to
receive you whenever you fincerely turn
to him — and, he is ready to aſſiſt you,
when you do but defire to obey him.—
Let your devotion then be the language
of filial love and gratitude—confide to
this kindeſt of Fathers every want, and
every wiſh of your heart;—but fubmit
them all to his will, and freely offer him
the difpofal of yourfelf, and of all your
affairs.—Thank him for his benefits, and
even for his puniſhments; — convinced
that thefe alfo are benefits, and mercifully
defigned for your good.—Implore his direction in all difficulties; his aſſiſtance in
all trials; his comfort and fupport in
ficknefs or affliction; his reſtraining grace
in the time ot profperity and joy.—Do
not perfiſt in defiring what his Providence
denies you; but be aſſured it is not good
for you—Refufe not any thing he allots
you, but embrace it as the beſt and pro-
pereſt for you.—Can you do lefs to your
heavenly Father than what your duty
to an earthly one requires?—If you were

A 5   to

to aſk permiſſion of your father, to do, or to have any thing you deſire, and he ſhould refuſe it to you, would you obſtinately perſiſt in ſetting your heart upon it, notwithſtanding his prohibition? would you not rather ſay, My father is wiſer than I am; he loves me, and would not deny my requeſt, if it was fit to be granted.—I will therefore baniſh the thought, and chearfully acquieſce in his will :—How much rather ſhould this be ſaid of our heavenly Father, whoſe wiſdom cannot be miſtaken, and whoſe bountiful kindneſs is infinite!—Love him therefore in the ſame manner you love your earthly parents, but in a much higher degree — in the higheſt your nature is capable of.— Forget not to dedicate yourſelf to his ſervice every day ;—to implore his forgiveneſs of your faults, and his protection from evil, every night : and this not merely in formal words, unaccompanied by any act of the mind, but " in ſpirit " and in truth ;" in grateful love, and humble adoration.—Nor let theſe ſtated periods of worſhip be your only communication

nication with him—accuſtom yourſelf to
think often of him, in all your waking
hours ;—to contemplate his wiſdom and
power, in the works of his hands ;—to
acknowledge his goodneſs in every object of uſe or of pleaſure ;—to delight in
giving him praiſe in your inmoſt heart,
in the midſt of every innocent gratification, — in the livelieſt hour of ſocial enjoyment.—You cannot conceive, if you
have not experienced, how much ſuch
ſilent acts of gratitude and love will enhance every pleaſure ; nor what ſweet
ſerenity and chearfulneſs ſuch reflections
will diffuſe over your mind. — On the
other hand, when you are ſuffering pain
or ſorrow, when you are confined to an
unpleaſant ſituation, or engaged in a
painful duty, how will it ſupport and animate you, to refer yourſelf to your almighty Father ! — to be aſſured that he
knows your ſtate and your intentions ;
that no effort of virtue is loſt in his ſight,
nor the leaſt of your actions or ſuffer
ings, diſregarded or forgotten !—that his
hand is ever over you, to ward off every
real

real evil, which is not the effect of your own ill conduct, and to relieve every suffering that is not useful to your future well-being!

You see, my dear, that true devotion is not a melancholy sentiment that depresses the spirits, and excludes the ideas of pleasure, which youth is so fond of: on the contrary, there is nothing so friendly to joy, so productive of true pleasure, so peculiarly suited to the warmth and innocency of a youthful heart. — Do not therefore think it too soon to turn your mind to God; but offer him the first-fruits of your understanding and affections: and, be assured, that the more you increase in love to him, and delight in his laws, the more you will encrease in happiness, in excellence, and honour: — that, in proportion as you improve in true piety, you will become dear and amiable to your fellow creatures; contented and peaceful in yourself; and qualified to enjoy the best blessings of this life, as well as to enherit the glorious promise of immortality.

Thus

Thus far have I fpoken of the firft principles of Religion : namely, belief in GOD, worthy notions of his attributes, and fuitable affections towards him,— which will naturally excite a fincere defire of obedience.—But, before you can obey his will, you muft know what that will is; you muft enquire in what manner he has declared it, and where you may find thofe laws, which muft be the rule of your actions.

The great laws of morality are indeed written in our hearts, and may be difcovered by reafon ; but our reafon is of flow growth ; very unequally difpenfed to different perfons ; liable to error, and confined within very narrow limits in all. If therefore, GOD has vouchfafed to grant a particular revelation of his will—if he has been fo unfpeakably gracious, as to fend his Son into the world to reclaim mankind from error and wickednefs— to die for our fins—and to teach us the way to eternal life;—furely it becomes us to receive his precepts with the deepeft reverence ; to love and prize them
above

above all things ; and to study them con-
stantly, with an earnest desire to conform
our thoughts, our words, and actions to
them.

As you advance in years and understanding, I hope you will be able to examine for yourself the evidences of the
Christian religion, and be convinced, on
rational grounds, of its divine authority.
—At present, such enquiries would demand more study, and greater powers
of reasoning, than your age admits of.
It is your part therefore, till you are capable of understanding the proofs, to believe your parents and teachers, that the
holy Scriptures are writings inspired by
God, containing a true history of facts,
in which we are deeply concerned — a
true recital of the laws given by God to
Moses ; and of the precepts of our blessed Lord and Saviour, delivered from his
own mouth to his disciples, and repeated
and enlarged upon in the edifying epistles
of his Apostles — who were men chosen
from amongst those who had the advantage of conversing with our Lord, to bear
witness

witneſs of his miracles and reſurrection—
and who, after his Aſcenſion, were aſ-
ſiſted and inſpired by the Holy Ghoſt.—
This ſacred volume muſt be the rule of
your life.—In it you will find all truths,
neceſſary to be believed; and plain and
eaſy directions, for the practice of every
duty: Your Bible then muſt be your
chief ſtudy and delight: but as it contains many various kinds of writing—
ſome parts obſcure and difficult of inter-
pretation, others plain and intelligible to
the meaneſt capacity—I would princi-
pally recommend to your frequent peruſal
ſuch parts of the holy writings as
are moſt adapted to your underſtanding,
and moſt neceſſary for your inſtruction.
Our Saviour's precepts were ſpoken to
the common people amongſt the Jews;
and were therefore given in a manner
eaſy to be underſtood, and equally ſtriking and inſtructive to the learned and
unlearned: for the moſt ignorant may
comprehend them, whilſt the wiſeſt muſt
be charmed and awed, by the beautiful
and majeſtic ſimplicity with which they

are

are expreffed. — Of the fame kind are the Ten Commandments, fpoken by God to Mofes; which, as they were defigned for univerfal laws, are worded in the moft concife and fimple manner, yet with a majefty which commands our utmoft reverence.

I think you will receive great pleafure, as well as improvement, from the hiftorical books of the Old Teftament — provided you read them as an hiftory, in a regular courfe, and keep the thread of it in your mind, as you go on. — I know of none, true or fictitious, that is equally wonderful, interefting, and affecting; or that is told in fo fhort and fimple a manner as this, which is, of all hiftories, the moft authentic.

In my next letter, I will give you fome brief directions, concerning the method and courfe I wifh you to purfue, in reading the holy Scriptures.—May you be enabled to make the beft ufe of this moft precious gift of God—this facred treafury of knowledge!—May you read the Bible, not as a tafk, nor as the dull

em-

employment of that day only, in which
you are forbidden more lively entertain-
ments — but, with a fincere and ardent
defire of inftruction; with that love and
delight in God's word, which the holy
Pfalmift fo pathetically felt and defcribed,
and which is the natural confequence of
loving God and virtue!—Though I fpeak
this of the Bible in general, I would not
be underftood to mean, that every part of
the volume is equally interefting. I have
already faid, that it confifts of various
matter, and various kinds of books,
which muft be read with different views
and fentiments. The having fome general notion of what you are to expect
from each book may poffibly help you
to underftand them, and heighten your
relifh of them—I fhall treat you as if you
were perfectly new to the whole; for fo
I wifh you to confider yourfelf; becaufe
the time and manner in which children
ufually read the Bible, are very ill cal-
culated to make them really acquainted
with it; and too many people who have
read it thus, without underftanding it in
their

their youth, satisfy themselves that they know enough of it, and never afterwards study it with attention, when they come to a maturer age.

Adieu, my beloved Niece! if the feelings of your heart, whilst you read my letters, correspond with those of mine, whilst I write them, I shall not be without the advantage of your partial affection, to give weight to my advice ; for believe me, my dear girl, my heart and my eyes overflow with tenderness, while I tell you, with how warm and earnest prayers for your happiness here, and hereafter, I subscribe myself,

your faithful friend

and most affectionate aunt.

L E T-

LETTER II.

I NOW proceed to give my dear niece some short sketches of the matter contained in the different books of the Bible—and of the course in which they ought to be read.

The first book, Genesis, contains the most grand, and, to us, the most interesting events that ever happened in the universe:—The creation of the world, and of man:—The deplorable fall of man, from his first state of excellence and bliss, to the distressed condition in which we see all his descendants continue:—The sentence of death pronounced on Adam, and on all his race—with the reviving promise of that deliverance, which has since been wrought for us, by our blessed Saviour:—The account of the early state of the world:—of the universal deluge: The division of mankind into different nations and languages:—The story of Abraham,

Abraham, the founder of the Jewish people, whose unshaken faith and obedience,
under the severest trial human nature
could sustain, obtained such favour in
the sight of God, that he vouchsafed to
stile him his friend, and promised to make
of his posterity a great nation ; and that
in his seed—that is, in one of his descendants—all the kingdoms of the earth
should be blessed : this, you will easily see,
refers to the Messiah, who was to be the
blessing and deliverance of all nations.—
It is amazing that the Jews, possessing this
prophecy, among many others, should
have been so blinded by prejudice, as to
expect, from this great personage, only a
temporal deliverance of their own nation
from the subjection to which they were
reduced under the Romans—it is equally
amazing, that some Christians should,
even now, confine the blessed effects of
his appearance upon earth, to this or that
particular sect or profession, when he is
so clearly and emphatically described as
the Saviour of the whole world.—The
story of Abraham's proceeding to sacri-
fice

fice his only fon at the command of God, is affecting in the higheft degree, and fets forth a pattern of unlimited refignation, that every one ought to imitate, in thofe trials of obedience under temptation, or of acquiefcence under afflicting difpenfations, which fall to their lot : of this we may be affured, that our trials will be always proportioned to the powers afforded us. — If we have not Abraham's ftrength of mind, neither fhall we be called upon to lift the bloody knife againft the bofom of an only child ;—but, if the almighty arm fhould be lifted up againft him, we muft be ready to refign him, and all we hold dear, to the divine will.— This action of Abraham has been cenfured by fome, who do not attend to the diftinction between obedience to a fpecial command, and the deteftably cruel facrifices of the Heathens, who fometimes voluntarily, and without any divine injunctions, offered up their own children, under the notion of appeafing the anger of their gods.—An abfolute command from God himfelf—as in the cafe of Abraham
—entirely

—entirely alters the moral nature of the action; fince he, and he only, has a perfect right over the lives of his creatures, and may appoint whom he will, either angel or man, to be his inftrument of deftruction. That it was really the voice of God which pronounced the command, and not a delufion, might be made certain to Abraham's mind, by means we do not comprehend, but which we know to be within the power of *him*, who made our fouls as well as bodies, and who can controul and direct every faculty of the human mind : — and we may be affured, that if he was pleafed to reveal himfelf fo miraculoufly, he would not leave a poffibility of doubting whether it was a real or an imaginary revelation :—thus the facrifice of Abraham appears to be clear of all fuperftition, and remains the nobleft inftance of religious faith and fubmiffion that was ever given by a mere man : — we cannot wonder that the bleffings beftowed on him for it, fhould have been extended to his pofterity —This book proceeds with the hiftory of Ifaac, which

becomes

becomes very interefting to us, from the touching fcene which I have mentioned — and ftill more fo, if we confider him as the type of our Saviour :—it recounts his marriage with Rebecca—the birth and hiftory of his two fons, Jacob, the father of the twelve tribes, and Efau, the father of the Edomites or Idumeans— the exquifitely affecting ftory of Jofeph and his brethren—and of his tranfplanting the Ifraelites into Egypt, who there multiplied to a great nation.

In EXODUS, you read of a feries of wonders, wrought by the Almighty, to refcue the oppreffed Ifraelites from the cruel tyranny of the Egyptians—who, having firft received them as guefts, by degrees reduced them to a ftate of flavery. By the moft peculiar mercies and exertions in their favour, God prepared his chofen people to receive, with reverent and obedient hearts, the folemn reftitution of thofe primitive laws, which probably he had revealed to Adam, and his immediate defcendants, or which, at leaft, he had made known by the dictates of confcience,

science, but which, time, and the dege-
neracy of mankind, had much obscured.
This important revelation was made to
them in the wilderness of Sinai : there,
assembled before the burning mountain,
surrounded " with blackness, and dark-
" ness, and tempest," they heard the
awful voice of God pronounce the eternal law, impressing it on their hearts with
circumstances of terror — but without
those encouragements and those excellent
promises, which were afterwards offered
to mankind by Jesus Christ. Thus were
the great laws of morality restored to the
Jews, and through them transmitted to
other nations ; and by that means a great
restraint opposed to the torrent of vice
and impiety, which began to prevail over
the world.

To those moral precepts, which are of
perpetual and universal obligation, were
superadded, by the ministration of Moses,
many peculiar institutions, wisely adapted to different ends — either, to fix the
memory of those past deliverances, which
were figurative of a future and far greater
salvation

falvation—to place inviolable barriers between the Jews and the idolatrous nations, by whom they were furrounded— or, to be the civil law, by which the community was to be governed.

To conduct this feries of events, and to eftablifh thefe laws with his people, God raifed up that great prophet Mofes, whofe faith and piety enabled him to undertake and execute the moft arduous enterprizes, and to purfue, with unabated zeal, the welfare of his countrymen :— even in the hour of death, this generous ardour ftill prevailed—his laft moments were employed in fervent prayers for their profperity, and, in rapturous gratitude, for the glimpfe vouchfafed him of a Saviour, far greater than himfelf, whom God would one day raife up to his people.

Thus did Mofes, by the excellency of his faith, obtain a glorious pre-eminence among the faints and prophets in heaven ; while, on earth, he will be ever revered, as the firft of thofe benefactors to mankind, whofe labours for the public good have endeared their memory to all ages.

B   The

The next book is LEVITICUS, which contains little befides the laws for the peculiar ritual obfervance of the Jews, and therefore affords no great inftruction to us now—You may pafs it over entirely ;— and, for the fame reafon, you may omit the firft eight chapters of NUMBERS.—The reft of Numbers is chiefly a continuation of the hiftory with fome ritual laws.

In DEUTERONOMY, Mofes makes a recapitulation of the foregoing hiftory, with zealous exhortations to the people, faithfully to worfhip and obey that God, who had worked fuch amazing wonders for them: he promifes them the nobleft temporal bleffings, if they prove obedient, with the moft awful and ftriking denunciations againft them, if they rebel, or forfake the true God.—I have before obferved, that the fanctions of the Mofaic law were *temporal* rewards and punifhments, thofe of the New Teftament are *eternal*—Thefe laft, as they are fo infinitely more forcible than the firft, were referved for the laft, beft gift to mankind
—and

—and were revealed by the Meſſiah, in the fulleſt and cleareſt manner.—Moſes, in this book, directs the method in which they were to deal with the ſeven nations, whom they were appointed to puniſh for their profligacy and idolatry ; and whoſe land they were to poſſeſs, when they had driven out the old inhabitants. He gives them excellent laws, civil as well as religious—which were ever after the ſtanding municipal laws of that people.— This book concludes with Moſes' ſong and death.

The book of Joshua contains the conqueſts of the Iſraelites over the ſeven nations, and their eſtabliſhment in the promiſed land.—Their treatment of theſe conquered nations muſt appear to you very cruel and unjuſt, if you conſider it as their own act, unauthorized by a poſitive command : but they had the moſt abſolute injunctions, not to ſpare theſe corrupt people—" to make no covenant with " them, nor ſhew mercy to them, but ut- " terly to deſtroy them."—And the reaſon is given—" leſt they ſhould turn

" away

" away the Ifraelites from following the
" Lord, that they might ferve other
" Gods *."—The children of Ifrael are
to be confidered as inftruments in the
hard of the Lord, to punifh thofe, whofe
idolatry and wickednefs had defervedly
brought deftruction on them :—this example, therefore, cannot be pleaded in
behalf of cruelty, or bring any imputation on the character of the Jews.—With
regard to other cities, which did not belong to thefe feven nations, they were directed to deal with them according to the
common law of arms at that time. If the
city fubmitted, it became tributary, and
the people were fpared.—If it refifted,
the men were to be flain, but the women
and children faved †. Yet, though the
crime of cruelty cannot be juftly laid to
their charge on this occafion, you will obferve, in the courfe of their hiftory, many
things recorded of them, very different
from what you would expect from the

* Deut. chap. ii.
† Deut. chap. xx.

chofen

chofen people of God, if you fuppofed
them felected on account of their own
merit : their national character was by no
means amiable—and, we are repeatedly
told, that they were not chofen for their
fuperior righteoufnefs—" for they were
" a ftiff-necked people, and provoked the
" Lord with their rebellions from the day
" they left Egypt."—" You have been
" rebellious againft the Lord, fays Mofes,
" from the day that I knew you.*"—
And he vehemently exhorts them, not to
flatter themfelves that their fuccefs was,
in any degree, owing to their own merits ;
—but they were appointed to be the
fcourge of other nations, whofe crimes
rendered them fit objects of divine cha-
ftifement.—For the fake of righteous
Abraham, their founder, and perhaps for
many other wife reafons, undifcovered to
us, they were felected from a world over-
run with idolatry, to preferve upon
earth the pure worfhip of the one only
God—and to be honoured with the birth

* Deut. chap. ix. ver. 24.

of the Meffiah amongft them—For this
end they were precluded, by divine command, from mixing with any other people, and defended by a great number of
peculiar rites and obfervances, from falling into the corrupt worfhip praĉtifed by
their neighbours.

The book of JUDGES—in which you
will find the affeĉting ftories of Sampfon
and of Jephtha—carries on the hiftory
from the death of Jofhua, about two
hundred and fifty years ;—but the faĉts
are not told in the times in which they
happened, which makes fome confufion ;
—and it will be neceffary to confult the
marginal dates and notes, as well as the
index, in order to get any clear idea of
the fucceffion of events, during that period.

The hiftory then proceeds regularly
through the two books of SAMUEL, and
thofe of KINGS : nothing can be more
interefting and entertaining than the
reigns of Saul, David, and Solomon—
but after the death of Solomon—when
ten tribes revolted from his fon Rehoboam
                                    and

and became a feparate kingdom—you
will find fome difficulty in underftanding
diftinctly the hiftories of the two kingdoms of Ifrael and Judah, which are
blended together, and, by the likenefs
of the names, and other particulars,
will be apt to confound your mind,
without great attention to the different
threads thus carried on together: —
The index here will be of great ufe
to you.—The fecond book of Kings concludes with the Babylonifh captivity, 588
years before Chrift—till which time, the
kingdom of Judah had defcended uninter-
ruptedly in the line of David.

The firft book of CHRONICLES begins
with a genealogy from Adam, through
all the tribes of Ifrael and Judah ; and the
remainder is the fame hiftory, which is
contained in the books of Kings, with
little or no variation, till the feparation
of the ten tribes :—From that period,
it proceeds with the hiftory of the kingdom of Judah alone, and gives therefore
a more regular and clear account of the
affairs of Judah than the book of Kings.

—You

—You may pafs over the firft book of Chronicles, and the nine firft chapters of the fecond book —but, by all means, read the remaining chapters, as they will give you more clear and diftinct ideas of the hiftory of Judah than that you read in the fecond book of Kings.—The fecond of Chronicles end, like the fecond of Kings, with the Babylonifh captivity.

You muft purfue the hiftory in the book of EZRA, which gives an account of the return of fome of the Jews, on the edict of Cyrus, and of the rebuilding the Lord's temple.

NEHEMIAH carries on the hiftory, for about twelve years, when he himfelf was governor of Jerufalem, with authority to rebuild the walls, &c.

The ftory of ESTHER is prior in time, to that of Ezra and Nehemiah ; as you will fee by the marginal dates ;—however, as' it happened during the feventy years captivity, and is a kind of epifode, it may be read in its own place.

This

This is the laft of the canonical books that is properly hiftorical; and I would therefore advife, that you pafs over what follows, till you have continued the hiftory through the apocryphal books.

The ftory of Job is probably very ancient, tho' it is a point on which learned men have differed :—It is dated, however, 1520 years before Chrift;—I believe it is uncertain by whom it was written :—many parts of it are obfcure, but it is well worth ftudying, for the extreme beauty of the poetry, and for the noble and fublime devotion it contains.— The fubjeƈt of the difpute between Job and his pretended friends, feems to be, whether the providence of God diftributes the rewards and punifhments of this life, in exaƈt proportion to the merit or demerit of each individual – His antagonifts fuppofe that it does; and therefore infer, from Job's uncommon calamities, that, notwithftanding his apparent righteoufnefs, he was in reality a grievous finner: —They aggravate his fuppofed guilt, by

B 5   the

the imputation of hypocrify, and call upon him to confefs it, and to acknowledge the juftice of his punifhment — Job afferts his innocence and virtue in the moft pathetic manner, yet does not prefume to accufe the fupreme Being of injuftice.— Elihu attempts to arbitrate the matter, by alledging the impoffibility that fo frail and ignorant a creature as man, fhould comprehend the ways of the Almighty, and, therefore, condemns the unjuft and cruel inference the three friends had drawn from the fufferings of Job. — He alfo blames Job for the prefumption of acquitting himfelf of all iniquity, fince the beft of men are not pure in the fight of God —but all have fomething to repent of— and he advifes him to make ufe of his afflictions.— At laft, by a bold figure of poetry, the fupreme Being himfelf is introduced, fpeaking from the whirlwind, and filencing them all, by the moft fublime difplay of his own power, magnificence, and wifdom, and of the comparative littlenefs and ignorance of man.— This indeed is the only conclufion of the
argument

argument that could be drawn, at a time when life and immortality were not yet brought to light.—A future retribution is the only fatisfactory folution of the difficulty arifing from the fufferings of good people in this life.

Next follow the PSALMS, with which you cannot be too converfant.—If you have any tafte, either of poetry or devotion, they will be your delight, and afford you a continual feaft.—The Bible tranflation is far better than that ufed in the Common-prayer Book ;—and will often give the fenfe, when the other is obfcure. —In this, as well as in all other parts of the Scripture, you muft be careful always to confult the margin, which gives you the corrections made fince the laft tranflation, and is often preferable to the words of the text.—I would wifh you to feleft fome of the Pfalms that pleafe you beft, and get them by heart; or, at leaft, make yourfelf miftrefs of the fentiments contained in them.—Dr. Delany's Life of David will fhew you the occafions on which feveral of them were compofed, which

which add much to their beauty and propriety—and by comparing them with the
events of David's life, you will greatly
enhance your pleafure in them.—Never
did the fpirit of true piety breathe more
ftrongly than in thefe divine fongs; which,
added to a rich vein of poetry, makes
them more captivating to my heart and
imagination, than any thing I ever read.
—You will confider how great difadvantages any poem muft fuftain from being
rendered literally into profe, and then
imagine how beautiful thefe muft be in
the original. — May you be enabled, by
reading them frequently, to transfufe into
your own breaft that holy flame which
infpired the writer!—To delight in the
Lord, and in his laws, like the Pfalmift—
to rejoice in him always, and to think,
" one day in his courts, better than a
" thoufand!"—But may you efcape the
heart-piercing forrow of fuch repentance
as that of David—by avoiding fin, which
humbled this unhappy king to the duft—
and which coft him fuch bitter anguifh, as
it is impoffible to read of without being
moved.

moved.—Not all the pleafures of the moft profperous finner, could counterbalance the hundredth part of thofe fenfations defcribed in his penitential Pfalms —and which muft be the portion of every man, who has fallen from a religious ftate into fuch crimes, when once he recovers a fenfe of religion and virtue, and is brought to a real hatred of fin :—however available fuch repentance may be to the fafety and happinefs of the foul after death, it is a ftate of fuch exquifite fuffering here, that one cannot be enough furprifed at the folly of thofe, who indulge in fin, with the hope of living to make their peace with God, by repentance.— Happy are they who preferve their innocence unfullied by any great or wilful crimes, and who have only the common failings of humanity to repent of—thefe are fufficiently mortifying to a heart fmitten with the love of virtue, and with the defire of perfection.—There are many very ftriking prophecies of the Meffiah, in thefe divine fongs ;—particularly in Pfalm xxii—fuch may be found fcattered

up

up and down almoft throughout the Old
Teftament.—To bear teftimony to *him*, is
the great and ultimate end, for which the
fpirit of prophecy was beftowed on the
facred writers:—but this will appear
more plainly to you, when you enter on
the ftudy of prophecy, which you are
now much too young to undertake.

The PROVERBS, and ECCLESIASTES,
are rich ftores of wifdom:—from which, I
wifh you to adopt fuch maxims as may be
of infinite ufe, both to your temporal and
eternal intereft.—But detached fentiments
are a kind of reading not proper to be
continued long at a time—a few of them,
well chofen and digefted, will do you
more fervice, than to read half a dozen
chapters together; in this refpect, they
are directly oppofite to the hiftorical
books, which, if not read in continuation,
can hardly be underftood, or retained to
any purpofe.

The SONG OF SOLOMON is a fine poem
—but its myftical reference to religion
lies too deep for a common underftanding: if you read it therefore, it will be
                                    rather

rather as matter of curiofity, than of edification.

Next follow the PROPHECIES, which, though highly deferving the greateft attention and ftudy, I think you had better omit for fome years—and then read them with a good expofition ; as they are much too difficult for you to underftand, without affiftance.—Dr. Newton on the Prophecies will affift you much, whenever you undertake this ftudy—which, you fhould by all means do, when your underftanding is ripe enough ; becaufe one of the main proofs of our religion refts on the teftimony of the Prophecies ; and they are very frequently quoted and referred to, in the New Teftament :—befides the fublimity of the language and fentiments—through all the difadvantages of antiquity and tranflation—muft, in many paffages, ftrike every perfon of tafte ; and the excellent moral and religious precepts found in them, muft be ufeful to all.

Though I have fpoken of thefe books, in order as they ftand, I repeat that they
are

are not to be read in that order—but that
the thread of the hiftory is to be purfued,
from Nehemiah, to the firft book of the
MACCABEES, in the Apocrypha; taking
care to obferve the Chronology regularly,
by referring to the Index, which fupplies
the deficiencies of this hiftory, from *Jofe-
phus's Antiquities of the Jews.*—The firft
carries on the ftory till within 195 years
of our Lord's circumcifion.—The fecond
book is the fame narrative, written by a
different hand, and does not bring the
hiftory fo far forward as the firft; fo that
it may be entirely omitted, unlefs you
have the curiofity to read fome particulars
of the heroic conftancy of the Jews, under
the tortures inflicted by their heathen conquerors, with a few other things not mentioned in the firft book.

You muft then connect the hiftory by
the help of the Index, which will give
you brief heads of the changes, that happened in the ftate of the Jews, from this
time, till the birth of the Meffiah.

The other books of the Apocrypha,
(though not admitted to be of facred authority)

thority) have many things well worthy of your attention, particularly the admirable book called ECCLESIASTICUS, and the BOOK OF WISDOM. But thefe muft be omitted in the courfe of reading which I advife, till after you have gone through the Gofpels and Acts, that you may not lofe the hiftorical thread.—I muft referve however what I have to fay to you, concerning the New Teftament, to another letter.

Adieu, my dear!

L E T-

L E T T E R III.

MY DEAREST NIECE,

WE come now to that part of Scripture, which is the moſt important
of all ; and which you muſt make your
conſtant ſtudy, not only till you are tho-
roughly acquainted with it, but all your
life long ; becauſe, how often ſoever repeated, it is impoſſible to read the life and
death of our bleſſed Saviour, without renewing and increaſing in our hearts, that
love, and reverence, and gratitude towards
him, which is ſo juſtly due for all he did,
and ſuffered for us! Every word that fell
from his lips, is more precious than all
the treaſures of the earth ; for his " are
" the words of eternal life!" They muſt
therefore be laid up in your heart, and be
conſtantly referred to, on all occaſions, as
the rule and direction of all your actions ;
particularly thoſe very comprehenſive moral

ral precepts he has gracioufly left with us, which can never fail to direct us aright, if fairly and honeftly applied : fuch as " *whatfoever you would that men fhould do* " *unto you, eevn fo do unto them.*"—There is no occafion, great or fmall, on which you may not fafely apply this rule, for the direction of your conduct; and, whilft your heart honeftly adheres to it, you can never be guilty of any fort of injuftice, or unkindnefs.—The two great commandments, which contain the fummary of our duty to God and man, are no lefs eafily retained and made a ftandard by which to judge our own hearts,—" *To love* " *the Lord our God, with all our hearts, with* " *all our minds, and with all our ftrength* ; " *and our neighbour* (or fellow creature) *as* " *ourfelves.*" " Love worketh no ill to his " neighbour," therefore if you have true benevolence, you will never do any thing injurious to individuals, or to fociety.— Now, all crimes whatever, are (in their remoter confequences, at leaft, if not immediately, and apparently) injurious to the fociety in which we live.—It is impoffible

fible *to love God*, without defiring to pleafe
him, and, as far as we are able, to refemble him; therefore the love of God muft
lead to every virtue in the higheft degree;
and, we may be fure, we do not truly
love him, if we content ourfelves with
avoiding flagrant fins, and do not ftrive,
in good earneft, to reach the greateft degree of perfection we are capable of.
Thus, do thofe few words direct us to the
higheft Chriftian virtue. — Indeed the
whole tenor of the gofpel is to offer us
every help, direction, and motive, that
can enable us to attain that degree of
perfection, on which depends our eternal
good.

What an example is fet before us in
our bleffed Mafter! How is his whole life,
from his earlieft youth, dedicated to the
purfuit of true wifdom, and to the practice of the moft exalted virtue? When
you fee him, at *twelve years of age,* in the
Temple, among the doctors, hearing
them, and afking them queftions, on the
fubject of religion — and aftonifhing them
all with his underftanding and anfwers —
you

you will fay perhaps,—" Well might the
" Son of God, even at thofe years, be far
" wifer than the aged ; but can a mortal
" child emulate fuch heavenly wifdom ?
" Can fuch a pattern be propofed to *my*
" imitation ?"—Yes, my dear ; remember that he has bequeathed you to his heavenly wifdom, as far as concerns your
good.   He has left you fuch declarations
of his will, and of the confequences of
your actions, as you are, even now, fully
able to underftand, if you will but attend
to them.— If then you will imitate his zeal
for knowledge, if you will delight in gaining information and improvement ; you
may even now become " *wife unto falva-*
" *tion.*"—Unmoved by the praife he acquired amongft thefe learned men, you
fee him meekly return to the fubjection of
a child under thofe who appeared to be
his parents, though he was in reality their
Lord :—you fee him return to live with
them, to work for them, and to be the
joy and folace of their lives ; till the time
came, when he was to enter on that fcene
of public action, for which his heavenly
Father

Father had fent him, from his own right
hand, to take upon him the form of a
poor carpenter's fon.—What a leffon of
humility is this, and of obedience to parents!—When, having received the glorious teftimony from heaven, of his being
the beloved Son of the moft High, he
enters on his public miniftry,—what an
example does he give us, of the moft extenfive and conftant benevolence!—how
are all his hours fpent in doing good to the
fouls and bodies of men!—not the meaneft finner is below his notice :—to reclaim
and fave them, he condefcends to converfe
familiarly with the moft corrupt, as well
as the moft abject.—All his miracles are
wrought to benefit mankind ; not one to
punifh and afflict them. —Inftead of ufing
the almighty power, which accompanied
him, to the purpofe of exalting himfelf,
and treading down his enemies, he makes
no other ufe of it, but to heal and to
fave.

When you come to read of his fufferings
and death, the ignominy and reproach,
the forrow of mind, and torment of body
which

which he fubmitted to! when you confider that it was all for our fakes—" that
by his ftripes we are healed,"—and by
his death we are raifed from deftruction
to everlafting life—what can I fay, that
can add any thing to the fenfations you
muft then feel ?—No power of language
can make the fcene more touching, than
it appears in the plain and fimple narra-
tions of the evangelifts ?—The heart that
is unmoved by it, can be fcarcely human :
—but, my dear, the emotions of tendernefs and compunction, which almoft every
one feels in reading this account, will be
of no avail, unlefs applied to the true
end;—unlefs it infpire you with a fincere
and warm affection towards your blefled
Lord—with a firm refolution to obey his
commands;—to be his faithful difciple;
—and ever renounce and abhor thofe fins,
which brought mankind under divine
condemnation, and from which we have
been redeemed, at fo dear a rate.—Remember that the title of Chriftian, or fol-
lower of Chrift, implies a more than ordi-
nary degree of holinefs and goodnefs.

As

As our motives to virtue are ſtronger than
thoſe which are afforded to the reſt of
mankind, our guilt will be proportionably
greater, if we depart from it.

Our Saviour appears to have had three
great purpoſes, in deſcending from his
glory, and dwelling amongſt men.—The
firſt to teach them true virtue, both by his
example and precepts.—The ſecond, to
give them the moſt forcible motives to
the practice of it by " bringing life and
" immortality to light :" by ſhewing
them the certainty of a reſurrection and
judgment, and the abſolute neceſſity of
obedience to God's laws.—The third,
to ſacrifice himſelf for us, to obtain by
his death the remiſſion of our ſins,—upon
our repentance and reformation—and the
power of beſtowing on his ſincere followers the ineſtimable gift of immortal happineſs.

What a tremendous ſcene does the
goſpel place before our eyes of the *laſt
day ?* —— When you, and every one
of us, ſhall awake from the grave, and
behold the Son of God, on his glorious
tribunal

tribunal, attended by millions of celeftial beings, of whofe fuperior excellence we can now form no adequate idea : When, in prefence of all mankind, of thofe holy angels, and of the great Judge himfelf, *you* muft give an account of your paft life, and hear your final doom, from which there can be no appeal, and which muft determine your fate to all eternity. —Then think—if for a moment you can bear the thought—what will be the defolation, fhame, and anguifh of thofe wretched fouls, who fhall hear thofe dreadful words;—" *Depart from me, ye* " *curfed, into everlafting fire, prepared for* " *the devil and his angels.*"—Oh!—my beloved child! —I cannot fupport even the idea of your becoming one of thofe undone, loft creatures!—I truft in GOD's mercy, that you will make a better ufe of that knowledge of his will, which he has vouchfafed you, and of thofe amiable difpo- fitions he has given you.—Let us therefore turn from this horrid, this infupportable view, and ftrive to imagine, as far as is poffible, what will be the fenfations of your foul, if you fhall hear our heavenly

C   judge

judge addrefs you in thefe tranfporting
words—" *Come, thou blefjed of my Father,*
" *inherit the kingdom prepared for you, from*
" *the foundation of the world.*"—Think,
what it muft be, to become an object of
the efteem and applaufe—not only of all
mankind affembled together—but of all
the hoft of heaven, of our blefjed Lord
himfelf—nay—of his and our almighty
Father ;—to find your frail flefh changed
in a moment into a glorious celeftial body, adorned with perfect beauty, health,
and agility—to find your foul cleanfed
from all its faults and infirmities; exalted to the pureft and nobleft affections
—overflowing with divine love and rapturous gratitude !—to have your underftanding enlightened and refined—your
heart enlarged and purified—and every
power, and difpofition of mind and body adapted to the higheft relifh of virtue
and happinefs!—Thus accomplifhed, to
be admitted into the fociety of amiable
and happy beings, all united in the moft
perfect peace and friendfhip, all breath-
ing nothing but love to God, and to
each

each other ; with them to dwell in scenes more delightful than the richest imagination can paint—free from every pain and care, and from all possibility of change or satiety : but above all, to enjoy the more immediate presence of GOD himself—to be able to comprehend and admire his adorable perfections in a high degree,—though still far short of their infinity—to be conscious of his love and favour, and to rejoice in the light of his countenance !—but here all imagination fails : — We can form no idea of that bliss, which may be communicated to us, by such a near approach to the source of all beauty and all good :—We must content ourselves with believing that it is what *mortal eye hath not seen, nor ear heard, neither hath it entered into the heart of man to conceive.*—The crown of all our joys will be to know that we are secure of possessing them for ever—without end !—What a transporting idea !

My dearest child ! can you reflect on all these things, and not feel the most earnest longings after immortality

—Do

—Do not all other views and defires feem
mean and trifling, when compared with
this ?—And does not your inmoft heart
refolve that this fhall be the chief and
conftant objeƌ of its wifhes and purfuit,
through the whole courfe of your life ?—
If you are not infenfible to that defire of
happinefs, which feems woven into our
nature, you cannot furely be unmoved
by the profpeƌ of fuch a tranfcendent degree of it ; and that, continued to all
eternity—perhaps continally increafing.
—You cannot but dread the forfeiture of
fuch an inheritance, as the moft infupportable evil !—Remember then — remember the conditions on which alone
it can be obtained.—God will not give
to vice, to carelefſnefs, or floth, the prize
he has propofed to virtue.—You have
every help that can animate your endeavours : —You have written laws to direƌ
you—the example of Chrift and his dif-
ciples to encourage you — the moft
awakening motives to engage you—and,
you have, befides, the comfortable promife

mife of conftant affiftance from the Holy
Spirit, if you diligently and fincerely pray
for it.—O, my dear child!—let not all
this mercy be loft upon you—but give
your attention to this your only important
concern, and accept, with profound gratitude, the ineftimable advantages that
are thus affectionately offered you.

Though the four gofpels are each of
them a narration of the life, fayings, and
death of Chrift; yet, as they are not exactly alike, but fome circumftances and
fayings, recorded in one, are omitted in
another, you muft make yourfelf perfectly
miftrefs of them all.

The Acts of the holy apoftles, en-
dowed with the Holy Ghoft, and autho-
rized by their divine Mafter, come next
in order to be read—Nothing can be
more interefting and edifying, than the
hiftory of their actions—of the piety,
zeal, and courage, with which they
preached the glad tidings of falvation—
and of the various exertions of the wonderful powers conferred on them by the
Holy Spirit, for the confirmation of their
miffion.

The

The character of St. Paul, and his miraculous converfion, demand your particular attention : moſt of the apoſtles were men of low birth and education ; but St. Paul was a Roman citizen ; that is, he poffeffed the privileges annexed to the freedom of the city of Rome, which was confidered as an high diſtinction in thofe countries, that had been conquered by the Romans.——He was educated amongſt the moſt learned fect of the Jews, and by one of their principal doctors.——He was a man of extraordinary eloquence, as appears not only in his writings, but in feveral fpeeches in his own defence, pronounced before governors and courts of juſtice, when called to account for the doctrines he taught.——He feems to have been of an uncommonly warm temper, and zealous in whatever religion he profeffed : this zeal, before his converfion, ſhewed itfelf in the moſt unjuſtifiable actions, by furiouſly perfecuting the innocent Chriſtians ; but, though his actions were bad, we may be fure his intentions were good ; otherwife we ſhould not have feen

a mia miracle employed to convince him of his miftake, and to bring him into the right-way.—This example may affure us of the mercy of God towards miftaken confciences, and ought to infpire us with the moft enlarged charity and good-will towards thofe, whofe erroneous principles miflead their conduct :—inftead of refentment and hatred againft their perfons, we ought only to feel an active wifh of affifting them to find the truth, fince we know not whether, if convinced, they might not prove, like St. Paul, chofen veffels to promote the honour of God, and of true religion. It is not my intention now to enter with you into any of the arguments for the truth of Chriftianity, otherwife it would be impoffible wholly to pafs over that which arifes from this remarkable converfion, and which has been fo admirably illuftrated by a noble writer *, whofe tract on this fubject is in every body's hands.

Next follow the EPISTLES, which make a very important part of the New Tefta-

* Lord Lyttelton.

ment;

ment ; and you cannot be too much employed in reading them.—They contain
the moſt excellent precepts and admonitions, and are of particular uſe in explain-
ing more at large ſeveral doctrines of
Chriſtianity, which we could not ſo fully
comprehend without them.—There are
indeed in the Epiſtles of St. Paul many
paſſages hard to be underſtood : Such, in
particular, are the firſt eleven chapters to
the Romans : the greater part of his Epiſtles to the Corinthians and Galatians : and
ſeveral chapters of that to the Hebrews.
— Inſtead of perplexing yourſelf with
theſe more obſcure paſſages of ſcripture,
I would wiſh you to employ your attention chiefly on thoſe that are plain ; and to
judge of the doctrines taught in the other
parts, by comparing them with what you
find in theſe.   It is through the neglect
of this rule, that many have been led to
draw the moſt abſurd doctrines from the
holy ſcriptures.—Let me particularly recommend to your careful peruſal the 12th,
13th, 14th, and 15th, chapters of the
Epiſtle to the Romans. In the 14th chap-
ter,

ter, St. Paul has in view the difference
between the Jewiſh and Gentile (or Heathen) converts at that time ;—the former
were diſpoſed to look with horror on the
latter, for their impiety in not paying the
ſame regard to the diſtinctions of days
and meats, that they did ; and the latter,
on the contrary, were inclined to look
with contempt on the former, for their
weakneſs and ſuperſtition.—Excellent is
the advice which the apoſtle gives to both
parties : he exhorts the Jewiſh converts
not to judge, and the Gentiles not to
deſpiſe—remembering that the kingdom
of heaven is not meat and drink, but
righteouſneſs, and peace, and joy in the
Holy Ghoſt :—Endeavour to conform
yourſelf to this advice ; to acquire a temper of univerſal candour and benevolence : and learn neither to deſpiſe nor
condemn any perſons on account of their
particular modes of faith and worſhip :
remembering always, that goodneſs is
confined to no party—that there are
wiſe and worthy men among all the ſects

C 5   of

of Chriftians—and that, to his own
mafter, every one muft ftand or fall.

I will enter no farther into the feveral
points difcuffed by St. Paul in his various
epiftles—moft of them too intricate for
your underftanding at prefent, and many
of them beyond my abilities to ftate clearly.—I will only again recommend to
you, to read thofe paffages frequently,
which, with fo much fervour and energy,
excite you to the practice of the moft exalted piety and benevolence.—If the ef-
fufions of a heart, warm'd with the tendereft affection for the whole human race
—if precept, warning, encouragement,
example, urged by an eloquence, which
fuch affection only could infpire, are capable of influencing your mind—you
cannot fail to find, in fuch parts of his
epiftles as are adapted to your underftanding, the ftrongeft perfuafions to every virtue that can adorn and improve your
nature.

The Epiftle of St. James is entirely
practical, and exceedingly fine; you cannot ftudy it too much.—It feems particularly

cularly defigned to guard Chriftians againft mifunderftanding fome things in St. Paul's writings, which have been fatally preverted to the encouragement of a dependance on faith alone, without good works.—But, the more rational commentators will tell you, that by the works of the law, which the apoftle afferts to be incapable of juftifying us, he means, not the works of moral righteoufnefs, but the ceremonial works of the Mofaic law ; on which the Jews laid the greateft ftrefs, as neceffary to falvation.—But, St. James tells us, that " if any man among us feem " to be religious, and bridleth not his " tongue, but deceiveth his own heart, " that man's religion is vain."—And that, " pure religion, and undefiled be- " fore God and the Father, is this, to " vifit the fatherlefs and widow in their " affliction, and to keep himfelf unfpotted " from the world." Faith in Chrift, if it produce not thefe effects, he declares is dead, or of no power.

The Epiftles of St. Peter are alfo full of the beft inftructions and admonitions, concerning

concerning the relative duties of life;
amongſt which are ſet forth the duties of
women in general, and of wives in particular.—Some part of his ſecond Epiſtle
is prophetical; warning the church of
falſe teachers, and falſe doctrines, which
ſhould undermine morality, and diſgrace
the cauſe of Chriſtianity.

The firſt of St. John is written in a
highly figurative ſtile, which makes it in
ſome parts hard to be underſtood: but,
the ſpirit of divine love which it ſo fervently expreſſes, renders it highly edifying and delightful.—That love of God
and of man, which this beloved apoſtle
ſo pathetically recommends, is in truth
the eſſence of religion, as our Saviour
himſelf informs us.

The book of REVELATIONS, contains
a prophetical account of moſt of the
great events relating to the Chriſtian
church, which were to happen from the
time of the writer, St. John, to the end
of the world.—Many learned men have
taken a great deal of pains to explain it;
and they have done this in many inſtances

very

very fuccefsfully ;—but I think it is yet
too foon for you to ftudy this part of fcripture : fome years hence perhaps there
may be no objection to your attempting
it, and taking into your hands the beft
expofitions to affift you in reading fuch of
the moft difficult parts of the New Teftament, as you cannot now be fuppofed
to underftand.—May heaven direct you
in ftudying this facred volume, and render it the means of making you wife unto
falvation !—May you love and reverence,
as it deferves, this bleffed and invaluable
book, which contains the beft rule of
life, the cleareft declaration of the will
and laws of the deity, the reviving affurance of favour to true penitents, and the
unfpeakably joyful tidings of eternal life
and happinefs to all the truly virtuous,
through Jefus Chrift, the Saviour and
Deliverer of the world.

Adieu.

L E T-

L E T T E R   IV.

YOU will have read the New Teftament to very little purpofe, my
deareft Niece, if you do not perceive the
great end and intention of all its precepts
to be the improvement and regulation of
the heart :—not the outward actions alone,
but the inward affections, which give
birth to them, are the fubjects of thofe
precepts : as appears in our Saviour's
explanation * of the commandments delivered to Mofes ; and in a thoufand other
paffages of the gofpels, which it is needlefs to recite. There are no virtues more
infifted on, as neceffary to our future
happinefs, than humility, and fincerity,
or uprightnefs of heart ; yet, none more
difficult and rare.—Pride and vanity—
the vices oppofite to humility—are the
fources of almoft all the worft faults, both
of men and women.—The latter are particularly

* Matth. v.

ticularly accufed—and not without reafon—of *vanity*, the vice of *little* minds,
chiefly converfant with trifling fubjects.
—Pride and vanity have been fuppofed
to differ fo effentially, as hardly ever to
be found in the fame perfon.—" Too
" proud to be vain," is no uncommon
expreffion — by which, I fuppofe, is
meant, too proud to be over anxious for
the admiration of others ; but this feems
to be founded on miftake.—Pride is, I
think, an high opinion of one's felf, and
an affected contempt of others : I fay,
affected, for that it is not a *real* contempt is
evident from this, that the loweft object
of it is important enough to torture the
proud man's heart, only by refufing him
the homage and admiration he requires.
—Thus Haman could relifh none of the
advantages on which he valued himfelf,
whilft that Mordecai, whom he pretended
to defpife, fat ftill in the king's gate, and
would not bow to him as he paffed.—
But as the proud man's contempt of others
is only affumed with a view to awe them
into reverence by his pretended fuperiority,

ty, fo it does not preclude an extreme inward anxiety about their opinions, and a flavifh dependance on them for all his gratifications : Pride—though a diftinct paffion—is feldom unaccompanied by vanity, which is an extravagant defire of admiration.—Indeed, I never faw an infolent perfon, in whom a difcerning eye might not difcover a very large fhare of vanity, and of envy, its ufual companion. —One may neverthelefs fee many *vain* perfons who are not *proud:* though they defire to be admired, they do not always admire themfelves; but as timid minds are apt to defpair of thofe things they earneftly wifh for, fo you will often fee the woman who is moft anxious to be thought handfome, moft inclined to be diffatisfied with her looks, and to think all the affiftance of art too little to attain the end defired.—To this caufe, I believe, we may generally attribute affectation ; which feems to imply a mean opinion of one's own real form, or character, while we ftrive againft nature to alter ourfelves by ridiculous contorfions of body, or by

feigned.

feigned fentiments and unnatural manners.—There is no art fo low, which
this mean paffion will not defcend to for
its gratification—no creature fo infignifi-
cant, whofe incenfe it will not gladly receive.—Far from defpifing others, the
vain man will court them with the moft
affiduous adulation ; in hopes, by feeding
their vanity, to induce them to fupply the
craving wants of his own. He will put on
the guife of benevolence, tendernefs and
friendfhip, where he feels not the leaft
degree of kindnefs, in order to prevail on
good nature and gratitude, to like and to
commend him : but if, in any particular
cafe, he fancies, that airs of infolence
and contempt may fucceed better, he
makes no fcruple to affume them ; though
fo aukwardly, that he ftill appears to depend on the breath of the perfon, he
would be thought to defpife. Weak and
timid natures feldom venture to try this
laft method ; and, when they do, it is
without the affurance neceffary to carry it
on with fuccefs : but, a bold and confi-
dent mind will oftener endeavour to command

mand and extort admiration than to court it.—As women are more fearful than men, perhaps this may be one reafon why they are more vain than proud ; whilft the other fex are oftener proud than vain. It is, I fuppofe, from fome opinion of a certain greatnefs of mind accompanying the one vice rather than the other, that many will readily confefs their pride, nay and even be proud of their pride, whilft every creature is afhamed of being con-victed of vanity. —You fee, however, that the end of both is the fame, though per-fued by different means; or, if it differ, it is in the impartance of the fubject.— Whilft men are proud of power, of wealth, dignity, learning, or abilities, young women are ufually ambitious of no-thing more than to be admired for their perfons, their drefs, or their moft trivial accomplifhments.—The homage of men is their grand object; but, they only defire them to be in love with their per-fons, carelefs how defpicable their minds appear, even to thefe their pretended adorers.—1 have known a woman fo vain

as

as to boaſt of the moſt diſgraceful addreſ-
ſes ; being contented to be thought
meanly of, in points the moſt intereſting to her honour, for the ſake of having
it known, that her perſon was attractive
enough to make a man tranſgreſs the
bounds of reſpect due to her character,
which was not a vicious one, if you except
this intemperate vanity.—But, this paſſion too often leads to the moſt ruinous
actions, always corrupts the heart, and,
when indulged, renders it, perhaps, as
diſpleaſing in the ſight of the Almighty, as
thoſe faults which find leaſt mercy from
the world ; yet alas! it is a paſſion ſo
prevailing, I had almoſt ſaid univerſal, in
our ſex, that it requires all the efforts of
reaſon, and all the aſſiſtance of grace, totally to ſubdue it.—Religion is indeed
the only effectual remedy for this evil.
—If our hearts are not dedicated to God,
they will in ſome way or other be dedicated to the world, both in youth and age.
— If our actions are not conſtantly referred to him, if his approbation and favour
be not our principal object, we ſhall certainly

tainly take up with the applaufe of men,
and make that the ruling motive of our
conduct.—How melancholy is it to fee
this phantom fo eagerly followed through
life! whilft all that is truly valuable to us is
looked upon with indifference; or, at beft,
made fubordinate to this darling perfuit!

Equally vain and abfurd is every fcheme
of life that is not fubfervient to, and does
not terminate in that great end of our
being—the attainment of real excellence,
and of the favour of God.—Whenever
this becomes fincerely our object, then
will pride and vanity, envy, ambition,
covetoufnefs, and every evil paffion, lofe
their power over us, and we fhall, in the
language of fcripture, " Walk humbly
" with our God."--We fhall then ceafe
to repine under our natural or accidental
difadvantages, and feel diffatisfied only
with our moral defects;—we fhall love
and refpect all our fellow creatures, as
the children of the fame dear parent,
and particularly thofe, who feek to do his
will: — " All our delight will be in the
faints that are in the earth, and in fuch
" as excel in virtue." We fhall wifh to
cultivate

cultivate good-will, and to promote innocent enjoyment wherever we are;—we
shall strive to please, not from vanity,
but from benevolence.—Instead of con-
templating our own fancied perfections,
or even real superiority with self-compla-
cence, religion will teach us to " look
" into ourselves, and fear :"—the best of
us, God knows, have enough to fear, if
we honestly search into all the dark reces-
ses of the heart, and bring out every
thought and intention fairly to the light,
to be tried by the precepts of our pure
and holy religion.

It is with the rules of the gospel we
must compare ourselves, and not with the
world around us ; for we know that the
" many are wicked ; and that we must
not be " conformed to the world."

How necessary it is, frequently thus to
enter into ourselves, and search out our
spirit, will appear, if we consider, how
much the human heart is prone to insince-
rity, and how often, from being first led
by vanity into attempts to impose upon
others, we come at last to impose on
ourselves.

There

There is nothing more common than to see people fall into the moſt ridiculous miſtakes, with regard to their own characters; but I can by no means allow ſuch miſtakes to be unavoidable, and therefore innocent. — They aroſe from voluntary inſincerity, and are continued for want of that ſtrict honeſty towards ourſelves and others, which the ſcripture calls "*ſingleneſs of heart*;" and which, in modern language, is termed *ſimplicity*—the moſt enchanting of all qualities, eſteemed and beloved in proportion to its rareneſs.

He, who "requires truth in the inward parts," will not excuſe our ſelf-deception; for he has commanded us to examine ourſelves diligently, and has given us ſuch rules as can never miſlead us, if we deſire the truth, and are willing to ſee our faults, in order to correct them.—But this is the point in which we are defective; we are deſirous to gain our own approbation, as well as that of others, at a cheaper rate than that of being really what we ought to be—and we take pains to perſuade ourſelves

felves that we are that which we indolently admire and approve.

There is nothing in which this felf-deception is more notorious, than in what regards fentiment and feeling.—Let a vain young woman be told that tendernefs and foftnefs are the peculiar charms of the fex—that even their weaknefs is lovely, and their fears becoming—and you will prefently obferve her grow fo tender as to be ready to weep for a fly; fo fearful, that fhe ftarts at a feather; and, fo weak-hearted, that the fmalleft accident quite overpowers her.—Her fondnefs and affection become fulfome and ridiculous; her compaffion grows contemptible weaknefs, and her apprehenfivenefs, the moft abject cowardice:—for, when once fhe quits the direction of nature, fhe knows not where to ftop, and continually expofes herfelf by the moft abfurd extremes.

Nothing fo effectually defeats its own ends, as this kind of affectation: for though warm affections and tender feelings are beyond meafure amiable and charming, when perfectly natural, and kept under the due controul of reafon and
                                    principle —

principle—yet nothing is fo truly difgufting as the affectation of them, or even
the unbridled indulgence of fuch as are
real.

Remember, my dear, that our feelings
were not given us for our ornament, but
to fpur us on to right actions—Compaffion, for inftance, was not impreffed upon
the human heart, only to adorn the fair
face with tears, and to give an agreeable
languor to the eyes—it was defigned to
excite our utmoft endeavours to relieve
the fufferer.—Yet, how often have I
heard that felfifh weaknefs, which flies
from the fight of diftrefs, dignified with
the name of tendernefs!—" My friend
" is, I hear, in the deepeft affliction and
" mifery;—I have not feen her—for
" indeed I cannot bear fuch fcenes—they
" affect me too much!—thofe who have
" lefs fenfibility are fitter for this world;
" —but, for my part, I own, I am not
" able to fupport fuch things.—I fhall
" not attempt to vifit her, till I hear
" fhe has recovered her fpirits."—This
have I heard faid with an air of com-
plaifance; and the poor felfifh creature
has

has perfuaded herfelf that fhe had finer feelings than thofe generous friends, who were fitting patiently in the houfe of mourning — watching, in filence, the proper moment to pour in the balm of comfort;—who fupprefled their own fenfations, and only attended to thofe of the afflicted perfon—and, whofe tears flowed in fecret, whilft their eyes and voice were taught to enliven the finking heart with the appearance of chearfulnefs.

That fort of tendernefs which makes us ufelefs, may indeed be pitied and excufed, if owing to natural imbecility— but, if it pretends to lovelinefs and excellence, it becomes truly contemptible.

The fame degree of active courage is not to be expected in woman as in man— and, not belonging to her nature, is not agreeable in her:—But paffive courage— patience, and fortitude under fufferings— prefence of mind, and calm refignation in danger—are furely defirable in every rational creature; efpecially in one profeffing to believe in an over-ruling Providence, in which we may at all times quietly confide, and which we may fafely truft

D with

with every event that does not depend
upon our own will.—Whenever you find
yourfelf deficient in thefe virtues, let it
be a fubject of fhame and humiliation—
not of vanity and felf-complacence:—do
not fancy yourfelf the more amiable for
that which really makes you defpicable—
but content yourfelf with the faults and
weakneffes that belong to you, without
putting on more by way of ornament —
With regard to tendernefs, remember
that compaffion is beft fhewn by an ardour
to relieve—and affection, by affiduity to
promote the good and happinefs of the
perfons you love:—that tears are unamiable, inftead of being ornamental, when
voluntarily indulged; and can never be
attractive but when they flow irrefiftibly,
and avoid obfervation as much as poffible:
—The fame may be faid of every other
mark of paffion.—It attracts our fympathy, if involuntary and not defigned for
our notice.—It offends, if we fee that it
is purpofely indulged, and obtruded on
our obfervation.

Another point, on which the heart is
apt

apt to deceive itfelf, is generofity :—we cannot bear to fufpect ourfelves of bafe and ungenerous feelings, therefore we let them work without attending to them, or we endeavour to find out fome better motive for thofe actions, which really flow from envy and malignity.—Before you flatter yourfelf that you are a generous benevolent perfon, take care to examine, whether you are really glad of every advantage and excellence, which your friends and companions poffefs, though they are fuch as you are yourfelf defective in. — If your fifter or friend makes a greater proficiency than yourfelf in any accomplifhment, which you are in purfuit of, Do you never wifh to ftop her progrefs, inftead of trying to haften your own ?

The boundaries between virtuous emulation and vicious envy, are very nice, and may be eafily miftaken.—The firft will awaken your attention to your own defects, and excite your endeavours to improve ; the laft will make you repine at the improvements of others, and wifh to rob them of the praife they have deferved.

—Do

—Do you fincerely rejoice when your
fifter is enjoying pleafure or commenda-
tion, though you are at the fame time in
difagreeable or mortifying circumftances?
—Do you delight to fee her approved and
beloved, even by thofe who do not pay
you equal attention?—Are you afflicted
and humbled, when fhe is found to be in
fault, though you yourfelf are remarkably
clear from the fame offence?—If your
heart affures you of the affirmative to
thefe queftions, then you may think yourfelf a kind fifter, and a generous friend:
for you muft obferve, my dear, that
fcarcely any creature is fo depraved, as
not to be capable of kind affections in
fome circumftances —We are all naturally
benevolent, when no felfifh intereft inter-
feres, and where no advantage is to be
given up :—we can all pity diftrefs, when
it lies complaining at our feet, and con-
feffes our fuperiority and happier fituation; but I have feen the fufferer himfelf
become the object of envy and ill-will, as
foon as his fortitude and greatnefs of mind
have begun to attract admiration, and to
make

make the envious perfon feel the fuperiority of virtue above good fortune.

To take fincere pleafure in the bleffings and excellencies of others, is a much furer mark of benevolence than to pity their calamities:—and you muft always acknowledge yourfelf ungenerous and felfifh, whenever you are lefs ready to "rejoice with them that do rejoice," than to "weep with them that weep."——If ever your commendations of others are forced from you, by the fear of betraying your envy, or if ever you feel a fecret defire to mention fomething that may abate the admiration given them, do not try to conceal the bafe difpofition from yourfelf, fince that is not the way to cure it.

Human nature is ever liable to corruption, and has in it the feeds of every vice, as well as of every virtue; and, the firft will be continually fhooting forth and growing up, if not carefully watched and rooted out as faft as they appear.—It is the bufinefs of religion to purify and exalt us, from a ftate of imperfection and infir-

D 3   mity,

mity, to that which is neceffary and effential to happinefs.——Envy would make us
miferable in Heaven itfelf, could it be admitted there; for we muft there fee beings
far more excellent, and confequently more
happy than ourfelves; and till we can rejoice in feeing virtue rewarded in proportion to its degree, we can never hope to
be among the number of the bleffed.

Watch then, my dear child, and obferve every evil propenfity of your heart,
that you may in time correct it, with the
affiftance of that grace, which alone can
conquer the evils of our nature, and which
you muft conftantly and earneftly implore.

I muft add, that even thofe vices which
you would moft blufh to own, and which
moft effectually defile and vilify the female heart, may by degrees be introduced
into yours—to the ruin of that virtue,
without which, mifery and fhame muft be
your portion—unlefs the avenues of the
heart are guarded by a fincere abhorrence
of every thing that approaches towards
evil.—Would you be of the number of
thofe

thofe bleffed, " who are pure in heart,"
— you muft hate and avoid every thing,
both in books and in converfation, that
conveys any impure ideas, however neatly
cloathed in decent language, or recommended to your tafte by pretended refine-
ments, and tender fentiments—by elegance of ftile, or force of wit or genius.

I muft not now begin to give you my
thoughts on the regulation of the affections, as that is a fubject of too much
confequence to be foon difmiffed—I fhall
dedicate to it my next letter; in the mean
time, believe me,

Your ever affectionate.

LET-

L E T T E R   III.

THE attachments of the heart, on which almoſt all the happineſs or miſery of life depends, are moſt intereſting objects of our conſideration.—I ſhall give my dear niece the obſervations which experience has enabled me to draw from real life and human nature, and not from what others have ſaid or written, however great their authority.

The firſt attachment of young hearts is *friendſhip*—the nobleſt and happieſt of affections, when real and built on a ſolid foundation;—but, oftener pernicious than uſeful to very young people, becauſe the connection itſelf is ill underſtood, and the ſubjects of it frequently ill choſen. Their firſt error is that of ſuppoſing equality of age, and exact ſimilarity of diſpoſition indiſpenſably requiſite in friends ; whereas, theſe are circumſtances which in a great meaſure diſqualify them for aſſiſting

each

each other in moral improvements, or fupplying each others defects ;— they ex-pofe them to the fame dangers, and in-cline them to encourage rather than cor-rect each other's failings.

The grand cement of this kind of friendfhip is telling fecrets, which they call confidence ;—and, I verily believe that the defire of having fecrets to tell, has often helped to draw filly girls into very unhappy adventures.—If they have no lover or amour to talk of, the too fre-quent fubject of their confidence is be-traying the fecrets of their families ; or conjuring up fancied hardfhips to com-plain of againft their parents or relations: this odious cabal, they call friendfhip ; and fancy themfelves dignified by the pro-feflion; but nothing is more different from the reality, as is feen by obferving how generally thofe early friendfhips drop off, as the parties advance in years and un-derftanding.

Do not you, my dear, be too ready to profefs a friendfhip with any of your young companions.—Love them, and be

always ready to ferve and oblige them,
and to promote all their innocent gratifications : but, be very careful how you
enter into confidences with girls of your
own age. — Rather choofe fome perfon of
riper years and judgment, whofe good-
nature and worthy principles may affure
you of her readinefs to do you fervice,
and of her candour and condefcenfion towards you.

I do not expect that youth fhould delight to affociate with age—or fhould lay
open its feelings and inclinations to fuch
as have almoft forgot what they were, or
how to make the proper allowance for
them ;—but if you are fortunate enough
to meet with a young woman eight or ten
years older than yourfelf, of good fenfe
and good principles, to whom you can
make yourfelf agreeable, it may be one
of the happieft circumftances of your life.
— She will be able to advife and improve
you—and, your defire of this affiftance
will recommend you to her tafte, as much
as her fuperior abilities will recommend
her to you —Such a connection will afford

you

you more pleafure, as well as more profit, than you can expect from a girl like your-felf, equally unprovided with knowledge, prudence, or any of thofe qualifications, which are neceffary to make fociety de-lightful.

With a friend, fuch as I have defcribed, of twenty-three or twenty-four years of age, you can hardly pafs an hour without finding yourfelf brought forwarder in fome ufeful knowledge—without learning fome-thing of the world, or of your own na-ture, fome rule of behaviour, or fome neceffary caution in the conduct of life :— for, even in the gayeft converfations, fuch ufeful hints may often be gathered from thofe, whofe knowledge and experience are much beyond our own.—Whenever you find yourfelf in real want of advice, or feek the relief of unburthening your heart, fuch a friend will be able to judge of the feelings you defcribe, or of the circumftances you are in—perhaps from her own experience—or at leaft, from the knowledge fhe will have gained of human nature ;—fhe will be able to point

out

out your dangers, and guide you into the
right path—or, if fhe finds herfelf incapable, fhe will have the prudence to direct
you to fome abler advifer.—The age I
have mentioned will not prevent her join-
ing in your pleafures, nor will it make her
a dull or grave companion ;—on the contrary, fhe will have more materials for
entertaining converfation, and her liveli-
nefs will fhew itfelf more agreeably than
in one of your own age. Your's therefore
will be the advantage in fuch a connection ; yet, do not defpair of being admitted into it, if you have an amiable and
docile difpofition. Ingenuous youth has
many charms for a benevolent mind—
and as nothing is more endearing than
the exercife of benevolence, the hope of
being ufeful and beneficial to you will
make her fond of your company.

I have known fome of the fweeteft and
moft delightful connections between perfons of different ages, in which the elder
has received the higheft gratification from
the affection and docility of the younger ;
whilft the latter has gained the nobleft advantages,

vantages, from the converſation and counſels of her wiſer friend.—Nor has the attachment been without uſe as well pleaſure, to the elder party.—She has found that there is no better way of improving one's own attainments than by imparting them to another; and the deſire of doing this in the moſt acceptable way, has added a ſweetneſs and gentleneſs to her manner, and taught her the arts of inſinuating inſtruction, and of winning the heart, whilſt ſhe convinces the underſtanding.

I hope, my dear, you in your turn will be this uſeful and engaging friend to your younger companions, particularly to your ſiſter and brothers, who ought ever—unleſs the ſhould prove unworthy—to be your neareſt and deareſt friends, whoſe intereſt and welfare you are bound to deſire as much as your own. If you are wanting here, do not fancy yourſelf qualified for friendſhip with others, but be aſſured, your heart is too narrow and ſelfiſh for ſo generous an affection.

Remember

Remember that the end of true friendfhip is the good of its object, and the
cultivation of virtue, in two hearts emu-
lous of each other, and defirous to perpe-
tuate their fociety beyond the grave.—
Nothing can be more contrary to this end
than that mutual intercourfe of flattery,
which fome call friendfhip.—A real friend
will venture to difpleafe me, rather than
indulge my faulty inclinations, and thereby increafe my natural frailties ;—fhe will
endeavour to make me acquainted with
myfelf, and will put me upon guarding
the weak parts of my character.

Friendfhip, in the higheft fenfe of the
word, can only fubfift between perfons of
ftrict integrity, and true generofity —Before you fancy yourfelf poffeffed of fuch a
treafure, you fhould examine the value of
your own heart, and fee how well it is
qualified for fo facred a connection :—and
then, a harder tafk remains—to find out
whether the object of your affection is
alfo endued with the fame virtuous difpofition.—Youth and inexperience are ill
able to penetrate into characters : the leaft
                                    appearance

appearance of good attracts their admiration, and they immediately suppose they have found the object they pursued.

It is a melancholy consideration that the judgment can only be formed by experience, which generally comes too late for our own use, and is seldom accepted for that of others.—I fear it is in vain for me to tell you what dangerous mistakes I made in the early choice of friends—how incapable I then was of finding out such as were fit for me, and how little I was acquainted with the true nature of friendship, when I thought myself most fervently engaged in it!—I am sensible all this will hardly persuade you to choose by the eyes of others, or even to suspect that your own may be deceived.—Yet, if you should give any weight to my observations, it may not be quite useless to mention to you some of the essential requisites in a friend; and to exhort you never to choose one in whom they are wanting.

The first of these is a deep and sincere regard to religion.—If your friend draws her principles from the same source with yourself—

yourſelf—if the goſpel precepts are the
rule of her life, as well as of yours, you
will always know what to expect from her,
and have one common ſtandard of right
and wrong to refer to, by which to regu-
late all material points of conduct. The
woman who thinks lightly of ſacred
things, or who is ever heard to ſpeak of
them with levity or indifference, cannot
reaſonably be expected to pay a more ſerious regard to the laws of friendſhip, or
to be uniformly punctual in the performance of any of the duties of ſociety:—
take no ſuch perſon to your boſom, however recommended by good humour, wit,
or any other qualification; nor let gaiety
or thoughtleſſneſs be deemed an excuſe for
offending in this important point: a perſon, habituated to the love and reverence
of religion and virtue, no more wants the
guard of ſerious conſideration to reſtrain
her from ſpeaking diſreſpectfully of them,
than to prevent her ſpeaking ill of her
deareſt friend. In the livelieſt hour of
mirth, the innocent heart can dictate nothing but what is innocent; it will immediately

diately take alarm at the apprehenſion of
doing wrong, and ſtop at once in the full
career of youthful ſprightlineſs, if re-
minded of the negleƈt or tranſgreſſion of
any duty—Watch for theſe ſymptoms of
innocence and goodneſs, and admit no
one to your entire affeƈtion, who would
ever perſuade you to make light of any ſort
of offence, or who can treat, with levity
or contempt, any perſon or thing that
bears a relation to religion.

A due regard to reputation is the next
indiſpenſible qualification.—" Have regard to thy name," ſaith the wiſe ſon of
Sirach, " for that will continue with thee
" above a thouſand great treaſures of
" gold."—The young perſon who is care-
leſs of blame, and indifferent to the
eſteem of the wiſe and prudent part of the
world, is not only a moſt dangerous companion, but gives a certain proof of the want
of reƈtitude in her own mind.—Diſcretion is the guardian of all the virtues;
and when ſhe forſakes them, they cannot
long reſiſt the attacks of an enemy.—
There is a profligacy of ſpirit in defying
the

the rules of decorum, and defpifing cen-
fure, which feldom ends otherwife than
in extreme corruption and utter ruin.—
Modefty and prudence are qualities that
early difplay themfelves, and are eafily
difcerned : where thefe do not appear,
you fhould avoid, not only friendfhip, but
every ftep towards intimacy, left your
own character fhould fuffer along with
that of your companion ; but, where
they fhine forth in any eminent degree,
you may fafely cultivate an acquaintance,
in the reafonable hope of finding the folid
fruits of virtue beneath fuch fweet and
promifing bloffoms : fhould you be difap-
pointed, you will at leaft have run no
rifque in the fearch after them, and may
cherifh as a creditable acquaintance the
perfon fo adorned, 'though fhe may not
deferve a place in your inmoft heart.

The underftanding muft next be exa-
mined :—and this is a point, which it requires fo much underftanding to judge of
in another, that I muft earneftly recommend to you, not to rely entirely upon
your own, but to take the opinion of your
older

older friends.—I do not wifh you to feek
for bright and uncommon talents, though
thefe are fources of inexhauftible delight
and improvement, when found in company with folid judgment and found principles.—Good fenfe (by which I mean a
capacity for reafoning juftly, and difcerning truly) applied to the ufes of life, and
exercifed in diftinguifhing charaƈters and
direƈting conduƈt, is alone *neceffary* to an
intimate conneƈtion; but without this, the
beft intentions—though certain of reward
hereafter—may fail of producing their
effeƈts in this life; nor can they fingly
conftitute the charaƈter of an ufeful and
valuable friend.—On the other hand, the
moft dazzling genius, or the moft engaging wit and humour, can but ill anfwer
the purpofes of friendfhip, without plain
common fenfe, and a faculty of juft reafoning.

What can one do with thofe who will
not be anfwered with reafon—and who,
when you are endeavouring to convince
or perfuade them by ferious argument, will
parry the blow with a witty repartee, or
a ftroke

a ftroke of poignant raillery ?—I know not
whether fuch a reply is lefs provoking than
that of an obftinate fool, who anfwers
your ftrongeft reafons with—" What you
" fay may be very true, but this is my
" way of thinking."—A fmall acquaint-
tance with the world will fhew you inftances of the moft abfurd and foolifh conduct, in perfons of brilliant parts and
entertaining faculties.—But, how trifling
is the talent of diverting an idle hour,
compared with true wifdom and prudence,
which are perpetually wanted to direct us
fafely and happily through life, and make
us ufeful and valuable to others !

Fancy, I know, will have her fhare, in
friendfhip, as well as in love ;—you muft
pleafe, as well as ferve me, before I can
love you as the friend of my heart.—But
the faculties that pleafe for an evening,
may not pleafe for life. —The humourous
man foon runs through his ftock of odd
ftories, mimickry, and jeft ; and the wit,
by conftantly repeated flafhes, confounds
and tires one's intellect, inftead of enli-
vening it with agreeable furprize :—but
good

good fenfe can neither tire nor wear out ;
—it improves by exercife—and increafes
in value, the more it is known :—the
pleafure it gives in converfation is lafting
and fatisfactory, becaufe it is accompanied
with improvement ;—its worth is proportioned to the occafion that calls for it, and
rifes higher on the moft interefting topics ;
—the heart as well as the underftanding,
finds its account in it ;— and our nobleft
interefts are promoted by the entertainment we receive from fuch a companion.

A good temper is the next qualification,
the value of which in a friend, you will
want no arguments to prove, when you
are truly convinced of the neceffity of it
in yourfelf, which I fhall endeavour to
fhew you in a following letter.—But, as
this is a quality in which you may be deceived, without a long and intimate acquaintance, you muft not be hafty in
forming connections, before you have had
fufficient opportunity for making obferva-
tions on this head.—A young perfon,
when pleafed and enlivened by the prefence of her youthful companions, feldom
fhews

ſhews ill temper; which muſt be extreme indeed, if it is not at leaſt controllable in ſuch ſituations.—But, you muſt watch her behaviour to her own family, and the degree of eſtimation ſhe ſtands in with them. — Obſerve her manner to ſervants and inferiors—to children—and even to animals. —See in what manner ſhe bears diſappointments, contradiction, and reſtraint; and what degree of vexation ſhe expreſſes on any accident of loſs or trouble.—If in ſuch little trials ſhe ſhews a meek, reſigned, and chearful temper, ſhe will probably preſerve it on greater occaſions; but if ſhe is impatient and diſcontented under theſe, how will ſhe ſupport the far greater evils which may await her in her progreſs through life?—If you ſhould have an opportunity of ſeeing her in ſickneſs, obſerve whether her complaints are of a mild and gentle kind—forced from her by pain, and reſtrained as much as poſſible—or whether they are expreſſions of a turbulent, rebellious mind, that hardly ſubmits to the Divine Hand.—See whether ſhe is tractable, conſiderate, kind,

and

and grateful to thofe about her; or whether fhe takes the opportunity which their compaffion gives her, to tyrannize over, and torment them.—Women are in general very liable to ill health, which muft neceffarily make them in fome meafure troublefome and difagreeable to thofe they live with.—They fhould therefore take the more pains to lighten the burden as much as poffible, by patience and good-humour; and be careful not to let their infirmities break in, on the health, freedom, or enjoyments of others, more than is needful and juft.—Some ladies feem to think it very improper for any perfon within their reach, to enjoy a moment's comfort while they are in pain; and make no fcruple of facrificing to their own leaft convenience, whenever they are indifpofed, the proper reft, meals, or refrefhments of their fervants, and even fometimes of their hufbands and children. —But their felfifhnefs defeats its own purpofe, as it weakens that affection and tender pity which excites the moft affiduous fervices, and affords the moft healing balm to the heart of the fufferer.

I have

I have already expreſſed my wiſhes that your choſen friend may be ſome years older than yourſelf ; but this is an advantage not always to be obtained.—Whatever be her age—*religion, diſcretion, good ſenſe,* and *good temper,* muſt on no account be diſpenſed with ; and, till you can find one ſo qualified, you had better make no cloſer connection than that of a mutual intercourſe of civilities and good offices.—But, if it is always your aim to mix with the beſt company, and to be worthy of ſuch ſociety, you will probably meet with ſome one among them deſerving your affection, to whom you may be equally agreeable.

When I ſpeak of the beſt company, I do not mean in the common acceptation of the world—perſons of high rank and fortune—but rather the moſt worthy and ſenſible. —It is however very important to a young woman to be introduced into life, on a reſpectable footing—and to converſe with thoſe, whoſe manners and ſtile of life may poliſh her behaviour, refine her ſentiments, and give her conſe-

quence

quence in the eye of the world. — Your equals in rank are moſt proper for intimacy, but, to be ſometimes amongſt your ſuperiors is every way deſirable and advantageous, unleſs it ſhould inſpire you with pride, or with the fooliſh deſire of emulating their grandeur and expence.

Above all things avoid intimacy with thoſe of low birth and education ; nor think it a mark of humility to delight in ſuch ſociety ; for it much oftener proceeds from the meaneſt kind of pride, that of being the head of the company, and ſeeing your companions ſubſervient to you. --The ſervile flattery and ſubmiſſion, which uſually recommend ſuch people, and make amends for their ignorance and want of converſation, will infallibly corrupt your heart, and make all company inſipid from whom you cannot expect the ſame homage. Your manners and faculties, inſtead of improving, muſt be continually lowered to ſuit you to your companions : and, believe me, you will find it no eaſy matter to raiſe them again to a

E   level

level with thofe of polite and well informed people.

The greateft kindnefs and civility to inferiors is perfectly confiftent with proper
caution on this head. — Treat them always with affability, and talk to them of
their own affairs, with an affectionate intereft; but never make them familiar,
nor admit them as affociates in your diverfions:—but above all, never truft them
with your fecrets, which is putting yourfelf entirely in their power, and fubjecting
yourfelf to the moft fhameful flavery. —
The only reafon for making choice of
fuch confidants muft be the certainty that
they will not venture to blame or contra-
dict inclinations, which you are confcious
no true friend would encourage. — But
this is a meannefs into which I truft you
are in no danger of falling. — I rather
hope you will have the laudable ambition
of fpending your time chiefly with thofe
whofe fuperior talents, education, and
politenefs, may continually improve you,
and whofe fociety will do you honour,
However let no advantage of this kind
weigh

weigh againſt the want of principle.—I
have long ago reſolved with David, that,
as far as lies in my power, " I will not
know a wicked perſon."—Nothing can
compenſate for the contagion of bad example, and for the danger of wearing off
by uſe, that horror and averſion from evil
actions and ſentiments, which every innocent mind ſets out with, but which an
indiſcriminate acquaintance in the world
ſoon abates, and at length deſtroys.

If you are good, and ſeek friendſhip
only amongſt the good, I truſt you will
be happy enough to find it.—The wiſe ſon
of Sirach pronounces that you will :—*
" A faithful friend," ſaith he, " is the
" medicine of life; and he that feareth
" the Lord ſhall find him. Whoſo feareth
" the Lord ſhall direct his friendſhip
" aright; for as he is, ſo ſhall his neigh-
" bour be alſo."—In the ſame admirable
book, you will find directions how to
chooſe and to preſerve a friend.—Indeed
there is hardly a circumſtance in life concerning which, you may not there meet

* Ecclus. vi.

with

with the beſt advice imaginable—Caution in making friendſhips is particularly recommended. —— * " Be in peace " with many, nevertheleſs have but one " counſellor of a thouſand. — If thou " wouldſt get a friend, prove him firſt, " and be not haſty to credit him; for " ſome man is a friend for his own occa- " ſion; and will not abide in the day of " trouble. And there is a friend who, be- " ing turned to enmity and ſtrife, will " diſcover thy reproach." — Again — " Some friend is a companion at the " table, and will not continue in the day " of thy afflicion; but in thy proſpe- " rity he will be as thyſelf, and will be " bold over thy ſervants: if thou be " brought low, he will be againſt thee, " and will hide himſelf from thy face."— " Chap. ix. 10 — " Forſake not an old " friend; for the new is not comparable " to him—A new friend is as new wine; " when it is old, thou ſhalt drink it with " pleaſure."

* Ecclus. vi.

When

When you have difcreetly chofen, the
next point is how to preferve your friend.
—Numbers complain of the ficklenefs and
ingratitude of thofe on whom they beftowed their affection ; but few examine
whether what they complain of, is not
owing to themfelves.—Affection is not
like a portion of freehold land, which
when once fettled upon you is a poffeffion
for ever, without further trouble on your
part.—If you grow lefs deferving, or
lefs attentive to pleafe, you muft expect
to fee the effects of your remiffnefs, in the
gradual decline of your friend's efteem
and attachment. — Refentment and reproaches will not recall what you have
loft : but, on the contrary, will haften
the diffolution of every remaining tie.—
The beft remedy is, to renew your care
and affiduity to deferve and cultivate affection, without feeming to have perceived its abatement.—Jealoufy and diftruft
are the bane of friendfhip, whofe effence
is efteem and affiance.—But if jealoufy
is expreffed by unkind upbraidings, or,
what is worfe, by cold, haughty looks and

E 3   infolent

infolent contempt, it can hardly fail, if
often repeated, to realize the misfortune,
which at firſt perhaps was imaginary.—
Nothing can be more an antidote to affection than ſuch behaviour, or than the
cauſe of it, which, in reality, is nothing
but pride; though the jealous perſon
would fain attribute it to uncommon tenderneſs and delicacy:—But tenderneſs
is never ſo expreſt; it is indeed deeply
ſenſible of unkindneſs, but it cannot be
unkind;—it may ſubſiſt with anger, but
not with contempt;—it may be weaken-
ed, or even killed, by ingratitude; but
it cannot be changed into hatred.—Remember always, that if you would be
loved, you muſt be *amiable*.—Habit may
indeed, for a time, ſupply the deficiency
of merit: what we have long loved, we
do not eaſily ceaſe to love; but habit will
at length be conquered by frequent diſ-
guſts.—" * Whoſo caſteth a ſtone at the
" birds, frayeth them away; and he that
" upbraideth his friend, breaketh friend-

* Ecclus. xxii. 20.

" ſhip.

" fhip. Though thou dreweft a fword at
" thy friend, yet defpair not, for there
" may be a returning to favour.—If thou
" haft opened thy mouth againft thy
" friend, fear not, for there may be a
" reconciliation ; except for *upbraiding,*
" or *pride,* or *difclofing of fecrets,* or a *trea-*
" *cherous wound,* — for, for thefe things
" every friend will depart."

I have hitherto fpoken of a friend in the
fingular number, rather in compliance
with the notions of moft writers, who have
treated of friendfhip, and who generally
fuppofe it can have but one objeƈt, than
from my own ideas.—The higheft kind
of friendfhip is indeed confined to one ;—
I mean the conjugal—which, in its per-
feƈtion, is fo entire and abfolute an union,
of intereft, will, and affeƈtion, as no other
conneƈtion can ftand in competition with.
—But, there are various degrees of
friendfhip, which can admit of feveral
objeƈts, efteemed, and delighted in, for
different qualities — and whofe feparate
rights are perfeƈtly compatible. — Perhaps it is not poffible to love two perfons
E 4   exaƈtly

exactly in the same degree; yet, the difference may be so small, that none of the
parties can be certain on which side the
scale preponderates.

It is a narrowness of mind to wish to
confine your friend's affection solely to
yourself; since you are conscious that
however perfect your attachment may be,
you cannot possibly supply to her all the
blessings she may derive from several
friends, who may each love her as well
as you do, and may each contribute
largely to her happiness.—If she depends
on you alone for all the comforts and advantages of friendship, your absence or
death may leave her desolate and forlorn.
—If therefore you prefer her good to your
own selfish gratification, you should rather
strive to multiply her friends, and be ready to embrace in your affections all who
love her, and deserve her love : this generosity will bring its own reward, by
multiplying the sources of your pleasures
and supports ; and your first friend will
love you the more for such an endearing
proof of the extent of your affection,
                                        which

which can ſtretch to receive all who are
dear to her. But if, on the contrary,
every mark of eſteem ſhewn to another
excites uneaſineſs or reſentment in you,
the perſon you love muſt ſoon feel her
connection with you a burden and reſtraint.—She can own no obligation to
ſo ſelfiſh an attachment; nor can her ten
derneſs be increaſed by that which leſſens
her eſteem.—If ſhe is really fickle and
ungrateful, ſhe is not worth your reproaches: if not, ſhe muſt be reaſonably
offended by ſuch injurious imputations.

You do not want to be told, that the
ſtricteſt fidelity is required in friendſhip:
and though poſſibly inſtances might be
brought, in which even the ſecret of a
friend muſt be ſacrificed to the calls of
juſtice and duty, yet theſe are rare and
doubtful caſes, and we may venture to
pronounce that " * Whoſo diſcovereth
" ſecrets, loſeth his credit, and ſhall ne-
" ver find a friend to his mind."—
" Love thy friend, and be faithful unto

* Ecclus. xxvii. 16

E 5   " him:

" him: but if thou bewrayeth his fecrets,
" follow no more after him.—For as a
" man that hath deftroyed his enemy,
" fo haft thou deftroyed the love of thy
" friend.—As one that letteth a bird go out
" of his hand, fo haft thou let thy neigh-
" bour go. — Follow no more after him,
" for he is too far off; he is as a roe ef-
" caped out of the fnare. — As for a
" wound it may be bound up; and after
" revilings there may be reconcilement;
" but he that bewrayeth fecrets, is with-
" out hope."

But in order to reconcile this inviolable
fidelity with the duty you owe to yourfelf
or others, you muft carefully guard againft
being made the repofitory of fuch fecrets
as are not fit to be kept.—If your friend
fhould engage in any unlawful perfuit—
if, for inftance, fhe fhould intend to carry
on an affair of love, unknown to her parents—you muft firft ufe your utmoft
endeavours to diffuade her from it;—
and, if fhe perfifts — pofitively and fo-
lemnly declare againft being a confidant
in fuch a cafe.—Suffer her not to fpeak

to

to you on the fubject, and warn her to for-
bear acquainting you with any ftep fhe
may propofe to take towards a marriage
unfanctified by parental approbation. —
Tell her, you would think it your duty
to apprize her parents of the danger into
which fhe was throwing herfelf.—However unkindly fhe may take this at the
time, fhe will certainly efteem and love
you the more for it, whenever fhe recovers a fenfe of her duty, or experiences
the fad effects of fwerving from it.

There is another cafe, which I fhould
not choofe to fuppofe poffible, in addreff-
ing myfelf to fo young a perfon, was it
not that too many inftances of it have of
late been expofed to public animadver-
fion : I mean the cafe of a married
woman, who encourages or tolerates the
addreffes of a lover.—May no fuch perfon be ever called a friend of yours! but
if ever one whom, when innocent, you
had loved, fhould fall into fo fatal an error, I can only fay that, after proper re-
monftrances, you muft immediately withdraw from all intimacy and confidence
with

with her.—Nor let the abſurd pretence
of *innocent intentions,* in ſuch circumſtances,
prevail with you to lend your countenance, a moment, to diſgraceful conduct.
—There cannot be innocence in any degree of indulgence to unlawful paſſion.
—The ſacred obligations of marriage are
very ill underſtood by the wife, who
can think herſelf innocent while ſhe par-
leys with a lover, or with love—and who
does not ſhut her heart and ears againſt
the moſt diſtant approaches of either.
—A virtuous wife—though ſhe ſhould
be ſo unhappy as not to be ſecured by
having her ſtrongeſt affections fixed on
her huſband—will never admit an idea
of any other man, in the light of a lover:
—but if ſuch an idea ſhould unawares in-
trude into her mind, ſhe would inſtantly
ſtifle it before it grew ſtrong enough to
give her much uneaſineſs.—Not to the
moſt intimate friend—hardly to her own
ſoul—would ſhe venture to confeſs a
weakneſs, ſhe would ſo ſincerely abhor:
—Whenever therefore ſuch infidelity of
heart is made a ſubject of confidence, depend upon it the corruption has ſpread far,
and has been faultily indulg'd.—Enter not
into

into her counfels :—Shew her the danger fhe is in, and then, vithdraw yourfelf from it, whilft you are yet unfullied by contagion.

It has been fuppofed a duty of friend-fhip to lay open every thought and every feeling of the heart to our friend.—But I have juft mentioned a cafe, in which this is not only unneceffary but wrong —A difgraceful inclination, which we refolve to conquer, fhould be concealed from every body ; and is more eafily fubdued when denied the indulgence of talking of its object :—and, I think, there may be other inftances, in which it would be moft prudent to keep our thoughts concealed even from our deareft friend.—Some things I would communicate to one friend, and not to another, whom per-haps I loved better, becaufe I might know that my firft friend was not fo well qualified as the other to counfel me on that particular fubject: a natural bias on her mind, fome prevailing opinion, or fome connection with perfons concerned, might make her an improper confidant with re-gard to one particular, though qualified to be fo, on all other occafions.

The

The confidence of friendſhip is indeed one of its ſweeteſt pleaſures and greateſt advantages. — The human heart often ſtands in need of ſome kind and faithful partner of its cares, in whom it may re- poſe all its weakneſſes, and with whom it is ſure of finding the tendereſt ſympathy. Far be it from me to ſhut up the heart with cold diſtruſt, and rigid caution, or to adopt the odious maxim, that " we " ſhould live with a friend, as if he were " one day to become an enemy."—But we muſt not wholly abandon prudence in any ſort of connection; ſince when every guard is laid aſide, our unbounded open- neſs may injure others as well as ourſelves. —Secrets entruſted to us muſt be ſacredly kept even from our neareſt friend—for we have no right to diſpoſe of the ſecrets of others.

If there is danger in making an impro- per choice of friends, my dear child, how much more fatal would it be to miſtake in a ſtronger kind of attachment—in that which leads to an irrevocable engagement for life ! yet ſo much more is the under- ſtanding blinded when once the fancy is captivated,

captivated, that it feems a defperate un-
dertaking, to convince a girl in love that
fhe has miftaken the character of the man
fhe prefers.

If the paffions would wait for the deci-
fion of judgment, and if a young woman
could have the fame opportunities of ex-
amining into the real character of her
lover, as into that of a female candidate
for her friendfhip, the fame rules might
direct you in the choice of both;—for,
marriage being the higheft ftate of friendfhip, the qualities requifite in a friend,
are ftill more important in a hufband.—-
But young women know fo little of the
world, efpecially of the other fex, and
fuch pains are ufually taken to deceive
them, that they are every way unqualified
to choofe for themfelves, upon their own
judgment.—Many a heart-ach fhall I feel
for you, my fweet girl, if I live a few
years longer!—Since, not only all your
happinefs in this world, but your advancement in religion and virtue, or your apo-
ftacy from every good principle you have
been taught, will probably depend on the
companion you fix upon for life.—Happy
will

will it be for you if you are wife and modeft enough to withdraw from temptation,
and preferve your heart free and open to
receive the juft recommendation of your
parents : farther than a recommendation
I dare fay they never will go, in an affair,
which, though it fhould be begun by
them, ought never to be proceeded in,
without your free concurrence.

Whatever romantic notions you may
hear, or read of, depend upon it, thofe
matches are almoft always the happieft
which are made on rational grounds—on
fuitablenefs of character, degree and fortune—on mutual efteem, and the profpect
of a real and permanent friendfhip.—
Far be it from me, to advife you to marry
where you do not love ;—a mercenary
marriage is a deteftable proftitution.—
But, on the other hand, an union formed
upon mere perfonal liking, without the
requifite foundation of efteem, without
the fanction of parental approbation, and
confequently, without the blefling of God,
can be productive of nothing but mifery
and fhame.—The paffion to which every
confideration of duty and prudence is fa-
crificed,

crificed, inftead of fupplying the lofs of
all other advantages, will foon itfelf be
changed into mutual diftruft – repentance
—reproaches—and finally perhaps into hatred.—The diftreffes it brings will be void
of every confolation :—you will have difgufted the friends who fhould be your fupport—debafed yourfelf in the eyes of the
world—and, what is much worfe, in your
own eyes; and even in thofe of your hufband—above all, you will have offended
that God, who alone can fhield you from
calamity.

From an act like this, I truft, your
duty and gratitude to your kind parents—
the firft duties next to that we owe to
God, and infeparably connected with it—
will effectually preferve you.—But moft
young people think they have fulfilled
their duty if they refrain from actually
marrying againft prohibition.—They fuffer their affections, and even perhaps their
word of honour to be engaged, without
confulting their parents : yet fatisfy themfelves with refolving not to marry without
their confent : not confidering that, befides the wretched, ufelefs, uncomfortable
ftate

ftate they plunge *themfelves* into, when they contract an hopelefs engagement, they likewife involve a *parent* in the miferable dilemma of either giving a forced confent againft his judgment, or of feeing his beloved child pine away her prime of life in fruitlefs anxiety—feeing her accufe him of tyranny, becaufe he reftrains her from certain ruin—feeing her affections alienated from her family – and all her thoughts engroffed by one object, to the deftruction of her health and fpirits, and of all her improvements and occupations.—What a cruel alternative for parents whofe happinefs is bound up with that of their child!—The time to confult them is before you have given a lover the leaft encouragement ; nor ought you to liften a moment to the man, who would wifh to keep his addreffes fecret; fince he thereby fhews himfelf confcious that they are not fit to be encouraged.

But perhaps I have faid enough on this fubject at prefent; though, if ever advice on fuch a topic can be of ufe, it muft be before paffion has got poffeffion of the heart, and filenced both reafon and principle.—

ciple.—Fix therefore in your mind as
deeply as poffible, thofe rules of duty and
prudence, which now feem reafonable to
you, that they may be at hand in the hour
of trial, and fave you from the miferies, in
which ftrong affections, unguided by difcretion, involve fo many of our fex.

If you love virtue fincerely, you will be
incapable of loving an openly vicious character.—But, alas!—your innocent heart
may be eafily enfnared by an artful one—
and from this danger nothing can fecure
you but the experience of thofe, to whofe
guidance God has entrufted you: may you
be wife enough to make ufe of it! So will
you have the faireft chance of attaining
the beft bleffings this world can afford,
in a faithful and virtuous union with a
worthy man, who may direct your fteps in
fafety and honour thro' this life, and par-
take with you the rewards of virtue in
that which is to come—But if this happy
lot fhould be denied you, do not be afraid
of a fingle life.—A worthy woman is never deftitute of friends, who in a great
meafure fupply to her the want of nearer
connections.—She can never be flighted
or

or difefteemed, while her good temper and benevolence render her a bleffing to her companions.—Nay, fhe muft be honoured by all perfons of fenfe and virtue, for preferring the fingle ftate to an union unworthy of her.—The calamities of an unhappy marriage are fo much greater than can befal a fingle perfon, that the unmarried woman may find abundant argument to be contented with her condition, when pointed out to her by Providence. —Whether married or fingle, if your firft care be to pleafe God, you will undoubtedly be a bleffed creature ;—" For " that which he delights in *muft be happy.*" How earneftly I wifh you this happinefs, you can never know, unlefs you could read the heart of

Your truly affectionate.

END OF THE FIRST VOLUME.

LETTERS

ON THE

IMPROVEMENT

OF THE

MIND.

ADDRESSED TO A YOUNG LADY.

I CONSIDER AN HUMAN SOUL WITHOUT EDU-
CATION, LIKE MARBLE IN THE QUARRY,
WHICH SHEWS NONE OF ITS INHERENT
BEAUTIES TILL THE SKILL OF THE POLISHER
FETCHES OUT THE COLOURS, MAKES THE
SURFACE SHINE, AND DISCOVERS EVERY
ORNAMENTAL CLOUD, SPOT AND VEIN THAT
RUNS THRO THE BODY OF IT. EDUCATION,
AFTER THE SAME MANNER, WHEN IT WORKS
UPON A NOBLE MIND, DRAWS OUT TO VIEW
EVERY LATENT VIRTUE AND PERFECTION,
WHICH WITHOUT SUCH HELPS ARE NEVER
ABLE TO MAKE THEIR APPEARANCE.
ADDISON.

VOLUME THE SECOND.

DUBLIN:

Printed for J. Exshaw, H. Saunders, W.
Sleater, J. Potts, D. Chamberlaine,
J. Williams, and R. Moncrieffe.
MDCCLXXIII.

LETTER VI.

THE next great point of importance to your future happiness, my dear, is what your parents have, doubtless, been continually attentive to from your infancy, as it is impossible to undertake it too early —I mean the due Regulation of your Temper. Though you are in a great measure indebted to their forming hands for whatever is good in it, you are sensible, no doubt, as every human creature is, of propensities to some infirmity of temper which it must now be *your own* care to correct and subdue ;—otherwise the pains that have hitherto been taken with you may all become fruitless : and, when you are your own mistress, you may relapse

into

into those faults, which were originally in your nature, and which will require to be diligently watched and kept under, thro' the whole course of your life.

If you consider, that the constant tenor of the Gospel precepts is to promote love, peace, and good-will amongst men, you will not doubt that the cultivation of an amiable disposition is a great part of your religious duty : since nothing leads more directly to the breach of charity, and to the injury and molestation of our fellow-creatures, than the indulgence of an ill temper.—Do not therefore think lightly of the offences you may commit, for want of a due command over it ; or suppose yourself responsible for them to your fellow creatures only ; but be assured, you must give a strict account of them all to the Supreme Governor of the world, who has made this a great part of your appointed trial upon earth.

A woman, bred up in a religious manner, placed above the reach of want, and out of the way of sordid or scandalous vices,

vices, can have but few temptations to the flagrant breach of the Divine Laws.—— It particularly concerns her, therefore, to underſtand them in their full import, and to conſider, how far ſhe treſpaſſes againſt them, by ſuch actions as appear trivial, when compared with murder, adultery, and theft, but which become of very great importance, by being frequently repeated, and occurring in the daily tranſ-actions of life.

The principal virtues or vices of a wo-man muſt be of a private and domeſtic kind.— Within the circle of her own fa-mily and dependants lies her ſphere of action— the ſcene of almoſt all thoſe taſks and trials, which muſt determine her cha-racter and her fate, both here, and here-after. — Reflect, for a moment, how much the happineſs of her huſband, chil-dren, and ſervants, muſt depend on her temper, and you will ſee that the greateſt good or evil, which ſhe ever may have in her power to do, may ariſe from her cor-recting or indulging its infirmities.

F   Though

Though I wish the principle of duty towards God to be your ruling motive in the exercise of every virtue, yet, as human nature stands in need of all possible helps, let us not forget how essential it is to present happiness, and to the enjoyment of this life, to cultivate such a temper as is indispensably requisite to the attainment of higher felicity in the life to come.— The greatest outward blessings cannot afford enjoyment to a mind ruffled and uneasy within itself.—A fit of ill humour will spoil the finest entertainment, and is as real a torment as the most painful disease. — Another unavoidable consequence of ill temper is the dislike and aversion of all who are witnesses to it, and, perhaps, the deep and lasting resentment of those who suffer from its effects.—We all, from social or self-love, earnestly desire the esteem and affection of our fellow creatures—and our condition makes them so necessary to us, that the wretch, who has forfeited them, must feel himself desolate and undone, deprived of all the best

enjoyments

enjoyments and comforts the world can afford, and given up to his inward mifery, unpitied and fcorned.—But this never can be the fate of a good-natured perfon:—whatever faults he may have, they will be treated with lenity—he will find an advocate in every human heart—his errors will be lamented rather than abhorred, and his virtues will be viewed in the faireft point of light:—His good humour, without the help of great talents or acquirements, will make his company preferable to that of the moft brilliant genius, in whom this quality is wanting:—in fhort, it is almoft impoffible that you can be fincerely beloved by any body, without this engaging property, whatever other excellencies you may poffefs; but, with it, you will fcarcely fail of finding fome friends and favourers, even though you fhould be deftitute of almoft every other advantage.

Perhaps you will fay, "all this is very "true, but our tempers are not in our "own power — we are made with dif-

"ferent

" ferent difpofitions, and, if mine be not
" amiable, it is rather my unhappinefs
" than my fault."—This, my dear, is
commonly faid by thofe who will not take
the trouble to correct themfelves.—Yet,
be affured, it is a delufion, and will not
avail in our juftification before Him,
" who knoweth whereof we are made,"
and of what we are capable. —It is true,
we are not all equally happy in our difpofitions—but human virtue confifts in che-
rifhing and cultivating every good inclination, and fabduing every propenfity to
evil. —If you had been born with a bad
temper, it might have been made a good
one, at leaft with regard to its outward
effects, by education, reafon, and principle :—and, though you are fo happy as
to have a good one while young, do not
fuppofe it will always continue fo, if you
neglect to maintain a proper command
over it. — Power, ficknefs, difapoint-
ments, or worldly cares, may corrupt and
embitter the fineft difpofition, if they
they are not counteracted by reafon and
religion.

It

It is obferved that every temper is inclined, in fome degree, either to paffion,
peevifhnefs, or obftinacy.—Many are fo
unfortunate as to be inclined to each of
the three in turn :—it is neceffary therefore to watch the bent of our nature, and
to apply the proper remedies for the infirmity to which we are moft liable.—With
regard to the firft, it is fo injurious to fociety, and fo odious in itfelf, efpecially in
the female character, that one fhould
think fhame alone would be fufficient to
preferve a young woman from giving way
to it; for it is as unbecoming her character
to be betrayed into ill behaviour by *paffion*
as by *intoxication*, and fhe ought to be
afhamed of one, as much as of the other.
—Gentlenefs, meeknefs, and patience,
are her particular diftinctions, and an en-
raged woman is one of the moft difgufting
fights in nature.

It is plain, from experience, that the
moft paffionate people can command
themfelves, when they have a motive fufficiently ftrong—fuch as the prefence of

F 3   thofe

thofe they fear, or to whom they particularly defire to recommend themfelves :—it is therefore no excufe to perfons, whom you have injured by unkind reproaches, and unjuft afperfions, to tell them you was in a paffion :—the allowing yourfelf to fpeak to them in paffion, is a proof of an infolent difrefpect, which the meaneft of your fellow creatures would have a right to refent.—When once you find yourfelf heated fo far as to defire to fay what you know would be provoking and wounding to another, you fhould immediately refolve rather to be filent, or to quit the room, than to give utterance to any thing dictated by fo bad an inclination.—Be affured, you are then unfit to reafon or to reprove, or to hear reafon from others.—It is therefore your part to retire from fuch an occafion of fin; and wait till you are cool, before you prefume to judge of what has paffed.—By accuftoming yourfelf thus to conquer and difappoint your anger, you will by degrees find it grow weak and manageable,

fo

fo as to leave your reafon at liberty :—
You will be able to reftrain your tougue
from evil, and your looks and geftures
from all expreffions of violence and ill-
will.—Pride, which produces fo many
evils in the human mind, is the great
fource of paffion.—Whoever cultivates
in himfelf a proper humility, a due fenfe
of his own faults and infufficiencies, and
a due refpect for others, will find but fmail
temptation to violent or unreafonable
anger.

In the cafe of real injuries, which juftify and call for refentment, there is a
noble and generous kind of anger, a proper and neceffary part of our nature,
which has nothing in it finful or degrad-
ing.—I would not wifh you infenfible to
this ; for the perfon, who feels not an injury, muft be incapable of being properly
affected by benefits.—With thofe, who
treat you ill without provocation, you
ought to maintain your own dignity.—
But, in order to do this, whilft you fhew
a fenfe of their improper behaviour, you

muft

muft preferve calmnefs, and even good breeding—and thereby convince them of the impotence as well as injuftice of their malice. You muft alfo weigh every circumftance with candour and charity, and confider whether your fhewing the refentment deferved may not produce ill confequences to innocent perfons—as is almoft always the cafe in family quarrels — and whether it may not occafion the breach of fome duty, or neceffary connection, to which you ought to facrifice even your juft refentments.—Above all things, take care that a particular offence to you does not make you unjuft to the general character of the offending perfon. —Generous anger does not preclude efteem from what ever is really eftimable, nor does it deftroy good-will to the perfon of its object :—It even infpires the defire of overcoming him by benefits—and wifhes to inflict no other punifhment than the regret of having injured one, who deferved his kindnefs :—it is always placable, and ready to be reconciled, as foon

as

as the offender is convinced of his error;
—nor can any subsequent injury provoke
it to recur to past disobligations, which
had been once forgiven.—But it is perhaps
unnecessary to give rules in this case:—
The consciousness of injured innocence
naturally produces dignity, and usually
prevents excess of anger.—Our passion is
most unruly, when we are conscious of
blame, and when we apprehend that we
have laid ourselves open to contempt. —
Where we know we have been wrong,
the least injustice in the degree of blame
imputed to us, excites our bitterest resentment; where we know ourselves faultless,
the sharpest accusation excites pity or contempt, rather than rage. — Whenever
therefore you feel yourself very angry,
suspect yourself to be in the wrong, and
resolve to stand the decision of your own
conscience before you cast upon another
the punishment which is perhaps due to
yourself.—This self-examination will at
least give you time to cool, and, if you
are just, will dispose you to balance your

own

own wrong with that of your antagonift, and to fettle the account with him on equal terms.

Peevifhnefs, though not fo violent and fatal in its immediate effects, is ftill more unamiable than paffion, and, if poffible, more deftructive of happinefs, in as much as it operates more continually. — Though the fretful man injures us lefs, he difgufts us more than the paffionate one—becaufe he betrays a low and little mind, intent on trifles, and engroffed by a paltry felf love, which knows not how to bear the very apprehenfion of any inconvenience. — It is felf love then, which we muft combat, when we find ourfelves affaulted by this infirmity; and, by voluntarily enduring inconveniencies, we fhall habituate ourfelves to bear them with eafe, and good-humour, when occafioned by others. — Perhaps this is the beft kind of religious mortification, as the chief end of denying ourfelves any innocent indulgences muft be to acquire a habit of command over our paffions and inclinations,

clinations, particularly fuch as are likely
to lead us into evil. — Another method
of conquering this enemy, is to abftract
our minds from that attention to trifling
circumftances, which ufually creates this
uneafinefs. — Thofe who are engaged in
high and important perfuits, are very
little affected by fmall inconveniencies.
— The man whofe head is full of ftudious
thought, or whofe heart is full of care,
will eat his dinner without knowing whether it was well or ill dreffed, or whether
it was ferved punctually at the hour or
not: and though abfence from the common things of life is far from defirable
— efpecially in a woman — yet too minute and anxious an attention to them
feldom fails to produce a teazing, mean,
and fretful difpofition. — I would therefore wifh your mind to have always fome
objects in perfuit worthy of it, that it
may not be engroffed by fuch as are in
themfelves fcarce worth a moment's anxiety. — It is chiefly in the decline of life,
when amufements fail, and when the
more

more importunate paſſions ſubſide, that
this infirmity is obſerved to grow upon us
—and perhaps it will ſeldom fail to do ſo,
unleſs carefully watched and counteracted by reaſon.—We muſt then endeavour
to ſubſtitute ſome perſuits in the place
of thoſe, which can only engage us in the
beginning of our courſe.—The perſuit of
glory and happineſs in another life, by
every means of improving and exalting
our own minds, becomes more and more
intereſting to us, the nearer we draw to
the end of all ſublunary enjoyments. —
Reading, reflection, rational converſation, and, above all, converſing with
God, by prayer and meditation, may preſerve us from taking that anxious intereſt
in the little comforts and conveniencies
of our remaining days, which uſually
gives birth to ſo much fretfulneſs in old
people.—But though the aged and infirm
are moſt liable to this evil—and they
alone are to be pitied for it—yet we
ſometimes ſee the young, the healthy,
and thoſe who enjoy moſt outward bleſ-

ſings,

fings, inexcufably guilty of it.—The fmalleft difappointment in pleafure, or difficulty in the moft trifling employment, will put wilful young people out of temper, and their very amufements frequently becomes fources of vexation and peevifhnefs.—How often have I feen a girl, preparing for a ball, or fome other public appearance — unable to fatisfy her own vanity — fret over every ornament fhe put on, quarrel with her maid, with her clothes, her hair; and growing ftill more unlovely as fhe grew more crofs, be ready to fight with her looking-glafs for not making her as handfome as fhe wifhed to be.—She did not confider that the traces of this ill humour on her countenance would be a greater difadvantage to her appearance than any defect in her drefs — or even than the plaineft features enlivened by joy and good humour. — There is a degree of refignation neceffary even to the enjoyment of pleafure;—we muft be ready and willing to give up fome part of what we could wifh for, before

fore we can enjoy that which is indulged to us. — I have no doubt that fhe, who frets all the while fhe is drefling for an af-fembly, will fuffer ftill greater uneafinefs when fhe is there. — The fame craving reftlefs vanity will there endure a thoufand mortifications, which, in the midft of feeming pleafure, will fecretly corrode her heart;—whilft the meek and hum-ble generally find more gratification than they expected, and return home pleafed and enlivened from every fcene of amufe-ment, though they could have ftaid away from it with perfect eafe and content-ment.

Sullennefs, or obftinacy, is perhaps a worfe fault of temper than either of the former — and, if indulged, may end in the moft fatal extremes of ftubborn melan-choly, malice, and revenge.—The refent-ment which, inftead of being exprefled, is nurfed in fecret, and continually aggra-vated by the imagination, will, in time, become the ruling paflion;—and then, how horrible muft be his cafe, whofe kind and

and pleaſurable affections are all ſwallow-
ed up by the tormenting as well as deteſta-
ble ſentiments of hatred and revenge!—
" * Admoniſh thy friend, peradventure
" he hath not done it : or if he hath, that
" he do it no more. — Admoniſh thy
" friend, peradventure he hath not ſaid
" it : or if he hath, that he ſpeak it not
" again."—Brood not over a reſentment,
which perhaps was at firſt ill grounded,
and which is undoubtedly heightened by
an heated imagination.—But, when you
have firſt ſubdued your own temper, ſo as
to be able to ſpeak calmly, reaſonably, and
kindly, then expoſtulate with the perſon
you ſuppoſe to be in fault — hear what
ſhe has to ſay ;—and either reconcile
yourſelf to her, or quiet your mind under
the injury, by the principle of Chriſtian
charity. — But if it ſhould appear that
you yourſelf have been moſt to blame,
or if you have been in an error, acknowledge it fairly and handſomely ;—if you

* Ecclus. xix. 13.

feel

feel any reluctance to do fo, be certain
that it arifes from pride, to conquer
which is an abfolute duty. — " A foft
" anfwer turneth away wrath," and a
generous confeffion oftentimes more than
atones for the fault which requires it.
— Truth and juftice demand that we
fhould acknowledge conviction, as foon as
we feel it—and not maintain an erroneous opinion, or juftify wrong conduct,
merely from the falfe fhame of confeffing
our paft ignorance.—A falfe fhame it undoubtedly is, and as impolitic as unjuft,
fince your error is already feen by thofe
who endeavour to fet you right;—but
your conviction, and the candour and
generofity of owning it freely, may ftill
be an honour to you, and a ftrong recommendation of you to the perfon with
whom you difputed. —With a difpofition
ftrongly inclined to fullennefs, or obftinacy, this muft be a very painful exertion;
and to make a perfect conqueft over
yourfelf at once, may perhaps appear im-
practicable, whilft the zeal of felf-juftifi-
cation,

cation, and the abhorrence of blame, are ftrong upon you.—But if you are fo unhappy as to yield to your infirmity, at the time, do not let this difcourage you from renewing your efforts.—Your mind will gain ftrength from the conteft, and your internal enemy will by degrees be forced to give ground.—Be not afraid to revive the fubject, as foon as you find yourfelf able to fubdue your temper; and then frankly lay open the conflict you fuftained at the time:—by this you will make all the amends in your power for your fault, and will certainly change the difguft you had given into pity at leaft, if not admiration.—Nothing is more endearing than fuch a confeffion:—and you will find fuch a fatisfaction in your own confcioufnefs, and in the renewed tendernefs and efteem you will gain from the perfon concerned, that your tafk for the future will be made more eafy, and your reluctance to be convinced, will on every occafion grow lefs and lefs.

The

The love of truth, and a real defire of improvement, ought to be the only motives of argumentation — and, where thefe are fincere, no difficulty can be made of embracing the truth, as foon as it is perceived. — But, in fact, people oftener difpute from vanity and pride, which make it a grievous mortification to allow that we are the wifer for what we have heard from another.—To receive advice, reproof, and inftruction, properly, is the fureft fign of a fincere and humble heart — and fhews a greatnefs of mind, which commands our refpect and reverence, while it appears fo willingly to yield to us the fuperiority.

Obferve, notwithftanding, that I do not wifh you to hear of your faults without pain: — Such an indifference would afford fmall hopes of amendment. — Shame and remorfe are the firft fteps to true repentance—yet we fhould be willing to bear this pain, and thankful to the kind hand that inflicts it for our good. —Nor muft we, by fullen filence un-

der

der it, leave our kind phyſician in doubt, whether the operation has taken effect or not, or whether it has not added another malady, inſtead of curing the firſt.—You muſt conſider, that thoſe who tell you of your faults, if they do it from motives of kindneſs and not of malice, exert their friendſhip in a painful office, which muſt have coſt them as great an effort, as it can be to you to acknowledge the ſervice; and, if you refuſe this encouragement, you cannot expect that any one, who is not abſolutely obliged to it by duty, will a ſecond time undertake ſuch an ill-re-quited trouble.—What a loſs would this be to yourſelf!—how difficult would be our progreſs to that degree of perfection which is neceſſary to our happineſs, was it not for the aſſiſtance we receive from each other!—this certainly is one of the means of grace held out to us by our merciful judge—and, if we reject it, we are anſwerable for all the miſcarriages we may fall into for want of it.

I know not, whether that ſtrange ca-price, that inequality of taſte and beha-viour,

viour, fo commonly attributed to our fex,
may be properly called a fault of temper
—as it feems not to be connected with,
or arifing from our animal frame, but to
be rather the fruit of our own felf-indul-
gence, degenerating by degrees into fuch
a wantonnefs of will as knows not how to
pleafe itfelf.—When inftead of regulating our actions by reafon and principle,
we fuffer ourfelves to be guided by every
flight and momentary impulfe of inclination, we fhall, doubtlefs, appear fo va-
riable and inconftant, that nobody can
guefs, by our behaviour to-day, what may
be expected from us to-morrow;—nor
can we ourfelves tell whether what we delighted in a week ago, will now afford us
the leaft degree of pleafure.—It is in vain
for others to attempt to pleafe us—we
cannot pleafe ourfelves, though all we wifh
for waits our choice:—and thus does a capricious woman become " fick of her-
" felf, through very felfifhnefs."—And,
when this is the cafe, it is eafy to judge
how fick others muft be of her, and how
                              contemptible

contemptible and difgufting fhe muft appear.—This wretched ftate is the ufual confequence of power and flattery.—May my dear child never meet with the temptation of that exceffive and ill judged indulgence from a hufband, which fhe has happily efcaped from her parents, and which feldom fails to reduce a woman to the miferable condition of an humoured child, always unhappy from having nobody's will to ftudy but its own.—The infolence of fuch demands for yourfelf, and fuch difregard to the choice and inclinations of others, can feldom fail to make you as many enemies as there are perfons obliged to bear with your humours — whilft a compliant, reafonable and contented difpofition, would render you happy in yourfelf, and beloved by all your companions—particularly by thofe, who live conftantly with you ; and of what confequence this is to your happinefs, a moment's reflection will convince you. — Family friendfhips are friendfhips made for us, if I may fo fpeak, by God himfelf.

felf.—With kindeſt intentions, he has
knit the bands of family love, by indiſ-
penſable duties ;—and wretched are they
who have burſt them aſunder by violence
and ill-will, or worn them out by conſtant
little diſobligations, and by the want of
that attention to pleaſe, which the preſence of a ſtranger always inſpires, but
which is often ſo ſhamefully neglected towards thoſe, whom it is moſt our duty
and intereſt to pleaſe.—May you, my
dear, be wiſe enough to ſee that every
faculty of entertainment, every engaging
qualification, which you poſſeſs, is exert-
ed to the beſt advantage for thoſe, whoſe
love is of moſt importance to you—for
thoſe who live under the ſame roof, and
with whom you are connected for life,
either by the ties of blood, or by the ſtill
more ſacred obligations of a voluntary
engagement.

To make you the delight and darling
of your family, ſomething more is required than barely to be exempt from ill
temper and troubleſome humours.—The
                                    ſincere

sincere and genuine smiles of complacency
and love, must adorn your countenance.
—That ready compliance, that alertness
to assist and oblige, which demonstrates
true affection, must animate your behaviour, and endear your most common
actions.—Politeness must accompany your
greatest familiarities, and restrain you
from every thing that is really offensive,
or which can give a moment's unecessary
pain.—Conversation, which is so apt to
grow dull and insipid in families, nay, in
some to be almost wholly laid aside, must
be cultivated with franknefs and open-
ness of friendship, and by the mutual communication of whatever may conduce to
the improvement or innocent entertainment of each other.

Reading, whether apart or in common,
will furnish useful and pleasing subjects—
and the sprightliness of youth will naturally inspire harmless mirth and native
humour, if encouraged by a mutual desire
of diverting each other, and making the
hours pass agreeably in your own house:
—every

—every amusement that offers will be heightened by the participation of these dear companions, and by talking over every incident together, and every object of pleasure.—If you have any acquired talent of entertainment, such as music, painting, or the like, your own family are those before whom you should most wish to excel, and for whom you should always be ready to exert yourself—not suffering the accomplishments you have gained, perhaps by their means, and at their expence, to lie dormant, till the arrival of a stranger gives you spirit in the performance. — Where this last is the case, you may be sure vanity is the only motive of the exertion.—A stranger will praise you more:—but how little sensibility has that heart, which is not more gratified by the silent pleasure painted on the countenance of a partial parent, or of an affectionate brother, than by the empty compliments of a visitor, who is perhaps inwardly more disposed to criticise and ridicule, than to admire you.

I have

I have been longer in this letter than I intended, yet it is with difficulty I can quit the fubject, becaufe I think it is feldom fufficiently infifted on, either in books or in fermons—and becaufe there are many perfons weak enough to believe themfelves in a fafe and innocent courfe of life, whilft they are daily haraffing every body about them, by their vexatious humours.—But, you will, I hope, conftantly bear in mind, that you can never treat a fellow creature unkindly, without offending the kind Creator and Father of all — and that you can no way render yourfelf fo acceptable to him, as by ftudying to promote the happinefs of others, in every inftance, fmall as well as great. —The favour of God, and the love of your companions, will furely be deemed rewards fufficient to animate your moft fervent endeavours – yet this is not all :— the difpofition of mind, which I would recommend, is its own reward, and is in itfelf effential to happinefs.— Cultivate it therefore, my dear child, with your utmoft diligence—and watch the fymptoms

G of

of ill-temper, as they rife, with a firm refolution to conquer them, before they are even perceived by any other perfon. —In every fuch inward conflict, call upon your Maker, to affift the feeble nature he he hath given you—and facrifice to *Him* every feeling that would tempt you to dif-obedience :—So will you at length attain that true Chriftian meeknefs, which is bleffed in the fight of God and man ; " which has the promife of this life, as " well as of that which is to come."— Then you will pity, in others, thofe in-firmities, which you have conquered in yourfelf ; — and will think yourfelf as much bound to affift, by your patience and gentlenefs, thofe who are fo unhappy as to be under the dominion of evil paf-fions, as you are to impart a fhare of your riches to the poor and miferable.

Adieu, my deareft.

LET-

LETTER VII.

MY DEAR NIECE,

OECONOMY is so important a part of a woman's character, so necessary to her own happiness, and so essential to her performing properly the duties of a wife and of a mother, that it ought to have the precedence of all other accomplishments, and take its rank next to the first duties of life.—It is nevertheless, an *art* as well as a *virtue*—and many well-meaning persons, from ignorance, or from inconsideration, are strangely deficient in it.—Indeed, it is too often wholly neglected in a young woman's education—and she is sent from her father's house to govern a family, without the least degree of that knowledge, which should qualify her for it :—this is the source of much

G 2 incon-

inconvenience:—for though experience
and attention may fupply, by degrees,
the want of inftruction, yet this requires
time—the family in the mean time may
get into habits, which are very difficult
to alter; and, what is worfe, the hufband's opinion of his wife's incapacity
may be fixed too ftrongly to fuffer him
ever to think juftly of her gradual improvements.—I would therefore earneftly advife you to make ufe of every opportunity
you can find, for laying in fome ftore of
knowledge or this fubject, before you are
called upon to the practice, by obferving
what paffes before you – by confulting
prudent and experienced miftreffes of families—and by entering in a book a me-
morandum of every new piece of intelli-
gence you acquire:—you may afterwards
compare thefe with more mature obferva-
tions, and make additions and corrections
as you fee occafion.—I hope it will not
be long before your mother entrufts you
with fome part, at leaft, of the management of your father's houfe.—Whilft you
are

are under her eye, your ignorance cannot do much harm, though the relief to her at firſt may not be near ſo conſiderable as the benefit to yourſelf.

Oeconomy conſiſts of ſo many branches, ſome of which deſcend to ſuch minute-neſſes, that it is impoſſible for me in writing to give you particular directions. —The rude outlines may perhaps be de-ſcribed, and I ſhall be happy if I can fur-niſh you with any hint that may hereafter be uſefully applied.

The firſt and greateſt point is to lay out your general plan of living in a juſt proportion to your fortune and rank:— if theſe two will not coincide, the laſt muſt certainly give way—for, if you have right principles, you cannot fail of being wretched under the ſenſe of the injuſtice as well as danger of ſpending beyond your income, and your diſtreſs will be con-tinually increaſing. — No mortifications, which you can ſuffer from retrenching in your appearance, can be comparable to this unhappineſs.—If you would enjoy the

real

real comforts of affluence, you fhould lay
your plan confiderably within your income, not for the pleafure of amaffing
wealth—though, where there is a growing family, it is an abfolute duty to lay by
fomething every year — but to provide
for contingencies, and to have the power
of indulging your choice in the difpofal of
the overplus—either in innocent pleafures
or to increafe your funds for charity and
generofity, which are in fact the true
funds of pleafure. — In fome circumftances indeed, this would not be prudent :—there are profeffions, in which a
man's fuccefs greatly depends on his making fome figure, where the bare fufpicion
of poverty would bring on the reality.—
—If, by marriage, you fhould be placed
in fuch a fituation, it will be your duty to
exert all your fkill in the management of
your income.—Yet, even in this cafe, I
would not ftrain to the utmoft for appearance, but would choofe my models among
the moft prudent and moderate of my
own clafs ; and be contented with flower
                    advancement,

advancement, for the fake of fecurity and peace of mind.

A contrary conduct is the ruin of many; and, in general, the wives of men in fuch profeffions might live in a more retired and frugal manner than they do, without any ill confequence, if they did not make the fcheme of advancing the fuccefs of their hufbands an excufe to themfelves for the indulgence of their own vanity and ambition.

Perhaps it may be faid, that the fettling the general fcheme of expences is feldom the wife's province, and that many men do not choofe even to acquaint her with the real ftate of their affairs.—Where this is the cafe, a woman can be anfwerable for no more than is entrufted to her. —But I think it a very ill fign, for one or both the parties, where there is fuch a want of opennefs, in what equally concerns them.—As I truft you will deferve the confidence of your hufband, fo I hope you will be allowed free confultation with him on your mutual interefts—and, I

G 4   believe,

believe, there are few men, who would not hearken to reason on their own affairs, when they saw a wife ready and desirous to give up her share of vanities and indulgences, and only earnest to promote the common good of the family.

In order to settle your plan, it will be necessary to make a pretty exact calculation:—and if, from this time, you accustom yourself to calculations in all the little expences entrusted to you, you will grow expert and ready at them, and be able to guess nearly, where certainty cannot be attained.—Many articles of expence are regular and fixed; these may be valued exactly. — And, by consulting with experienced persons, you may calculate nearly the amount of others :— any material article of consumption, in a family of any given number and circumstances, may be estimated pretty nearly. —Your own expences of clothes and pocket-money should be settled and circumscribed, that you may be sure not to exceed the just proportion.—I think it an

excellent

excellent method to appropriate fuch a portion of your income, as you judge proper to beftow in charity, to be facredly kept for that purpofe, and no longer con- fidered as your own.— By which means, you will avoid the temptation of giving lefs than you ought, through felfifhnefs, or more than you ought, through good- nature or weaknefs.—If your circumftan- ces allow it, you might fet apart another fund for acts of liberality or friendfhip, which do not come under the head of charity.—The having fuch funds ready at hand makes it eafy and pleafant to give —and, when acts of bounty are perform ed, without effort, they are generally done more kindly and effectually.—If you are obliged in confcience to lay up for a family, the fame method of an appro- priated fund for faving will be of excel- lent ufe, as it will prevent that continual and often ineffectual anxiety, which a ge- neral defire of faving, without having fixed the limits, is fure to create.

G 5   Regularity

Regularity of payments and accounts, is effential to Oeconomy :—your houfe-keeping fhould be fettled at leaft once a week, and all the bills paid :—all other tradefmen fhould be paid, at fartheft, once a year.—Indeed I think it more advantageous to pay oftener:—but, if you make them truft you longer, they muft either charge proportionably higher, or be lofers by your cuftom. — Numbers of them fail, every year, from the cruel caufe of being obliged to give their cuftomers fo much longer credit than the dealers from whom they take their goods, will allow to them.—If people of fortune confidered this, they would not defer their payments, from mere negligence, as they often do, to the ruin of whole families.

You muft endeavour to acquire fkill in purchafing ;—and, in order to this, you fhould take every opportunity of learning the real value of every thing, as well as the marks whereby you are to diftinguifh the good from the bad.

In

In your table—as in your drefs, and in
all other things, I wifh you to aim at
propriety and *neatnefs* — or, if your ftate
demands it, *elegance* — rather than *fuper-
fluous figure*—To go beyond your fphere,
either in drefs, or in the appearance of
your table, indicates a greater fault in
your character than to be too much within
it. — It is impoffible to enter into the
minutiæ of the table:—good fenfe, and
obfervation on the beft models, muft form
your tafte, and a due regard to what you
can afford, muft reftrain it.

Ladies, who are fond of needle-work,
generally choofe to confider that as a principal part of good houfewifery: — and,
though I cannot look upon it as of equal
importance with the due regulation of a
family, yet, in a middling rank, and
with a moderate fortune, it is a neceffary
part of a woman's duty, and a confiderable article in expence is faved by it.—
Many young ladies make almoft *every
thing* they wear — by which means they
can make a genteel figure at a fmall expence—

pence. — This, in your ſtation, is the moſt profitable and deſirable kind of work ;—and, as much of it as you can do, conſiſtently with a due attention to your health, to the improvement of your mind, and to the diſcharge of other duties, I ſhould think highly commendable. —But as I do not wiſh you to impoſe on the world by your appearance, I ſhould be contented to ſee you worſe dreſſed, rather than ſee your whole time employed in preparations for it — or any of thoſe hours given to it, which are needful to make your body ſtrong and active by exerciſe, or your mind rational by reading. — Abſolute idleneſs is inexcuſable in a woman, becauſe the needle is always at hand for thoſe intervals, in which ſhe cannot be otherwiſe employed.—If you are induſtrious, and if you keep good hours, you will find time for all your proper employments. — Early riſing, and a good diſpoſition of time, is eſſential to œconomy. The neceſſary orders, and examination into houſhold affairs, ſhould be

disfpatched,

difpatched, as foon in the day, and as
privately as poffible, that they may not
interrupt your hufband or guefts, or break
in upon converfation, or reading, in the
remainder of the day.—If you defer any
thing that is neceffary, you may be tempt-
ed by company, or by unforefeen avoca-
tions to forget, or to neglect it: hurry
and irregularity will enfue, with expen-
five expedients to fupply the defect.

There is in many people, and particularly in youth, a ftrange averfion to regularity—a defire to delay what ought to be
done immediately, in order to do fomething elfe, which might as well be done
afterwards. —Be affured, it is of more
confequence to you than you can conceive,
to get the better of this idle procraftinat-
ing fpirit and to acquire habits of conftancy and fteadinefs, even in the moft
trifling matters : — without them there
can be no regularity, or confiftency of
action or character — no dependance on
your beft intentions, which a fudden humour may tempt you to lay afide for a
time—

time — and which a thoufand unforefeen accidents will afterwards render it more difficult to execute: — no one can fay what important confequences may follow a trivial neglect of this kind. — For example—I have known one of thefe *pro-craftinators* difoblige, and gradually lofe very valuable friends, by delaying to write to them fo long, that, having no good excufe to offer, fhe could not get courage enough to write at all, and drop-ped their correfpondence entirely.

The neatnefs and order of your houfe and furniture, is a part of œconomy which will greatly affect your appearance and character, and to which you muft yourfelf give attention, fince it is not pof-fible even for the *rich* and *great* to rely wholly on the care of fervants, in fuch points, without their being often neglect-ed.—The more magnificently a houfe is furnifhed, the more one is difgufted with that air of confufion, which often pre-vails where attention is wanting in the owner.—But, on the other hand, there
is

is a kind of neatneſs, which gives a lady
the air of a houſe-maid, and makes her
exceſſively troubleſome to every body,
and particularly to her huſband :—in this,
as in all branches of œconomy, I wiſh
you to avoid all parade and buſtle.—
Thoſe ladies, who pique themſelves on
the particular excellence of neatneſs, are
very apt to forget that the decent order of
of a houſe ſhould be deſigned to promote
the convenience and pleaſure of thoſe who
are to be in it—and that, if it is convert-
ed into a cauſe of trouble and conſtraint,
their huſbands and gueſts would be happier without it.—The love of fame, that
univerſal paſſion, will ſometimes ſhew itſelf on ſtrangely inſignificant ſubjects ; and
a perſon, who acts for praiſe only, will
always go beyond the mark in every
thing.—The beſt ſign of a houſe being
well governed is that nobody's attention
is called to any of the little affairs of it,
but all goes on ſo well of courſe that one
is not led to make remarks upon any
thing, nor to obſerve any extraordinary
effort

effort that produces the general refult of eafe and elegance, which prevails throughout.

Domeftic œconomy, and, the credit and happinefs of a family, depend fo much on the choice and proper regulation of fervants, that it muft be confidered as an effential part both of prudence and duty. — Thofe, who keep a great number of them, have a heavy charge on their confciences, and ought to think themfelves in fome meafure refponfible for the morals and happinefs of fo many of their fellow-creatures, defigned like themfelves for immortality.—Indeed the cares of domeftic management are by no means lighter to perfons of high rank and fortune, if they perform their duty, than to thofe of a retired ftation. A family, like a commonwealth, the more numerous and luxurious it becomes, the more difficult it is to govern it properly.—Though the great are placed above the little attentions and employments, to which a private gentlewoman muft dedicate much

of

of her time, they have a larger and more important fphere of action, in which, if they are indolent and neglectful, the whole government of their houfe and fortune muft fall into irregularity.—Whatever number of deputies they may employ to overlook their affairs, they muft themfelves overlook thofe deputies, and be ultimately anfwerable for the conduct of the whole.—The characters of thofe fervants, who are entrufted with power over the reft, cannot be too nicely enquired into; and the miftrefs of the family muft be ever watchful over their conduct —at the fame time that fhe muft carefully avoid every appearance of fufpicion, which whilft it wounds and injures a worthy fervant, only excites the artifice and cunning of an unjuft one.

None, who pretend to be friends of religion and virtue, fhould ever keep a domeftic, however expert in bufinefs, whom they know to be guilty of immorality.—How unbecoming a ferious character is it, to fay of fuch a one, " he is a
" bad

" bad man, but a good fervant!"—
What a preference does it fhew of private
convenience to the interefts of fociety,
which demand that vice fhould be conftantly difcountenanced, efpecially in every
one's own houfhold ; and that the fober,
honeft, and induftrious, fhould be fure of
finding encouragement and reward, in the
houfes of thofe who maintain refpectable
characters.—Such perfons fhould be in-
variably ftrict and peremptory with regard
to the behaviour of their fervants, in
every thing which concerns the general
plan of domeftic government—but fhould
by no means be fevere on fmall faults,
fince nothing fo much weakens authority
as frequent chiding. — Whilft they require precife obedience to their rules,
they muft prove by their general conduct,
that thefe rules are the effect, not of humour, but, of reafon. — It is wonderful
that thofe, who are careful to conceal their
ill-temper from ftrangers, fhould be indifferent how peevifh and even contemptibly
capricious they appear before their fervants,

vants, on whom their good-name fo much
depends, and from whom they can hope
for no real refpect, when their weaknefs is
fo apparent.—When once a fervant can
fay—" I cannot do any thing to pleafe
" my miftrefs to-day,"—all authority is
loft.

Thofe, who continually change their
fervants, and complain of perpetual ill-
ufage, have good reafon to believe that
the fault is in themfelves, and that they
do not know how to govern.—Few indeed poffefs the fkill to unite authority
with kindnefs, or are capable of that ftea-
dy and uniformly reafonable conduct,
which alone can maintain true dignity,
and command a willing and attentive obedience—Let us not forget that human
nature is the fame in all ftations.—If you
can convince your fervants, that you have
a generous and confiderate regard to their
health, their intereft, and their reafonable
gratifications—that you impofe no commands but what are fit and right, nor
ever reprove but with juftice and temper.
—Why

—Why fhould you imagine that they
will be infenfible to the good they receive,
or whence fuppofe them incapable of
efteeming and prizing fuch a miftrefs?—I
could never, without indignation, hear it
faid that "fervants have no gratitude,"—
as if the condition of fervitude excluded
the virtues of humanity!—The truth is,
mafters and miftreffes have feldom any
real claim to gratitude. — They think
highly of what they beftow, and little of
the fervice they receive :—they confider
only their own convenience, and feldom
reflect on the kind of life their fervants
pafs with them—they do not afk themfelves, whether it is fuch an one as is confiftent with the prefervation of their health,
their morals, their leifure for religious duties, or with a proper fhare of the enjoyments and comforts of life.—The diffipated manners, which now fo generally
prevail, perpetual abfence from home,
and attendance on affemblies, or at public
places, are, in all thefe refpects, pernicious
to the whole houfhold—and to the *men*
                                    fervants

fervants abfolutely ruinous.—Their only
refource, in the tedious hours of waiting,
whilft their mafters and ladies are engaged in diverfions, is to find out fomething
of the fame fort for themfelves.—Thus
are they led into gaming, drinking, extravagance, and bad company—and
thus, by a natural progreffion, they become diftreft and difhoneft.—That attachment and affiance, which ought to
fubfift between the dependant and his
protector, are deftroyed. — The mafter
looks on his attendants as thieves and
traitors, whilft they confider him as one,
whofe money only gives him power over
them—and, who ufes that power, without the leaft regard to their welfare.

   * " The fool faith—I have no friends
" —I have no thanks for all my good
" deeds, and they that eat my bread fpeak
" evil of me."—Thus foolifhly do thofe
complain, who choofe their fervants, as well
as their friends, without difcretion, or who

    * Ecclus. xx. 16.

treat

treat them in a manner that no worthy
perſon will bear.

I have been often ſhocked at the want
of politeneſs, by which maſters and miſ-
treſſes ſometimes provoke impertinence
from their ſervants :—a gentleman who
would reſent to death, an imputation of
falſehood from his equal, will not ſcruple
without proof, to accuſe his ſervant of it,
in the groſſeſt terms.—I have heard the
moſt inſolent contempt of the whole claſs
expréſſed at a table, whilſt five or ſix of
them attended behind the chairs, who,
the company ſeemed to think, were without ſenſes, without underſtanding or natural feelings of reſentment: — theſe are
cruel injuries, and will be retorted in ſome
way or other.

If you, my dear, live to be at the head
of a family, I hope you will not only
avoid all injurious treatment of your do-
meſtics, but behave to them with that
courteſy which will heighten their reſpect,
as well as their affection. — If on any occaſion, they do more than you have a right
to require, give them, at leaſt, the reward
of

of feeing that they have obliged you.—
if, in your fervice, they have any hardfhip
to endure, let them fee that you are concerned for the neceffity of impofing it.—
When they are fick, give them all the attention, and every comfort in your power,
with a free heart and kind countenance ;
" * not blemifhing thy good deeds, nor
" ufing uncomfortable words, when thou
" giveft any thing. — Is not a word
" better than a gift ?—but both are with
" a gracious man !—A fool will upbraid
" churlifhly, and a gift of the envious
" confumeth the eyes."

Whilft you thus endear yourfelf to all
your fervants, you muft ever carefully
avoid making a favourite of any ;—unjuft diftinctions, and weak indulgences to
one, will of courfe excite envy and hatred
in the reft. Your favourite may eftablifh
whatever abufes fhe pleafes—none will
dare to complain againft her, and you
will be kept ignorant of her ill practices
—but will feel the effects of them, by

* Ecclus. xviii.

finding

finding all your other fervants uneafy in
their places, and perhaps by being obliged continually to change them.

When they have fpent a reafonable
time in your fervice, and have behaved
commendably, you ought to prefer them,
if it is in your power—or to recommend
them to a better provifion.—The hope of
this keeps alive attention and gratitude,
and is the proper fupport of induftry.—
Like a parent, you fhould keep in view
their eftablifhment in fome way, that may
preferve their old age from indigence;
and, to this end, you fhould endeavour to
infpire them with care to lay up part of
their gains, and conftantly difcourage in
them all vanity in drefs and extravagance
in idle expences.—That you are bound
to promote their eternal as well as temporal welfare, you cannot doubt, fince
next to your children they are your near-
eft dependants.—You ought therefore to
inftruct them as far as you are able, furnifh them with good books fuited to their
capacity, and fee that they attend the public

lic worſhip of God ; — and you muſt take
care ſo to paſs the ſabbath-day as to allow
them time, on that day at leaſt, for reading and reflection at home, as well as for
attendance at church.—Though this is a
part of your religious duty, I mention it
here, becauſe it is alſo a part of family
management : — for the ſame reaſon, I
ſhall here take occaſion earneſtly to recommend family prayers, which are uſeful to all, but moſt particularly to ſervants
—who, being conſtantly employed, are
led to the neglect of private prayer and
whoſe ignorance makes it very difficult
for them to frame devotions for themſelves, or to chooſe proper helps amidſt
the numerous books of ſuperſtitious or
enthuſiaſtic nonſenſe, which are printed
for that purpoſe.—Even, in a political
light, this practice is eligible, ſince the
idea, which it will give them of your regularity and decency, if not counter-act-
ed by other parts of your conduct, will
probably increaſe their reſpect for you,
and will be ſome reſtraint, at leaſt on

H   their

their outward behaviour, though it fhould fail of that inward influence, which in general may be hoped from it.

The prudent diftribution of your charitable gifts may not improperly be confidered as a branch of Oeconomy, fince the great duty of alms-giving cannot be truly fulfilled without a diligent attention fo to manage the fums you can fpare as to produce the moft real good to your fellow creatures.—Many are willing to give money, who will not beftow their time and confideration, and who therefore often hurt the community, when they mean to do good to individuals.—The larger are your funds, the ftronger is the call upon you to exert your induftry and care in difpofing of them properly —It feems impoffible to give rules for this, as every cafe is attended with a variety of circumftances that muft all be confidered. In general, charity is moft ufeful, when it is appropriated to animate the induftry of the young, to procure fome eafe and comforts to old age, and to fupport in ficknefs

nefs thofe whofe daily labour is their only
maintenance in health.—They, who are
fallen into indigence, from circumftances
of eafe and plenty, and in whom education and habit have added a thoufand
wants to thofe of nature, muft be confidered with the tendereft fympathy, by
every feeling heart.—To fuch, it is needlefs to fay that the bare fupport of exiftence is fcarcely a benefit—and that the
delicacy and liberality of the manner, in
which relief is here offered, can alone
make it a real act of kindnefs.—In great
families, the wafte of provifions, fufficient
for the fupport of many poor ones, is a
fhocking abufe of the gifts of providence.
—Nor fhould any lady think it beneath
her to ftudy the beft means of prevent-
ing it, and of employing the refufe of luxury in the relief of the poor. Even the
fmalleft families may give fome affiftance
in this way, if care is taken that nothing
be wafted.

I am fenfible, my dear child, that very
little more can be gathered from what I

have

have faid on Oeconomy, than the general
importance of it, which cannot be too
much impreffed on your mind — fince
the natural turn of young people is to neglect and even defpife it, not diftinguifhing it from parfimony and narrownefs of
fpirit. But be affured, my dear, there
can be no true generofity without it —
that the moft enlarged and liberal mind
will find itfelf not debafed but ennobled
by it.—Nothing is more common than
to fee the fame perfon, whofe want of Oeconomy is ruining his family, confumed
with regret and vexation at the effect of
his profufion; and, by endeavouring to
fave, in fuch trifles as will not amount to
20 pounds in a year, that which he waftes
by hundreds, incur the character and
fuffer the anxieties of a mifer, together
with the misfortunes of a prodigal.—A
rational plan of expence will fave you from
all thefe corroding cares, and will give
you the full and liberal enjoyment of what
you fpend.—An air of eafe, of hofpitality
and franknefs will reign in your houfe,
                                        which

which will make it pleafant to your friends and to yourfelf.—" Better is a " morfel of bread," where this is found, than the moft elaborate entertainment, with that air of conftraint and anxiety, which often betrays the grudging heart through all the difguifes of civility.

That you, my dear, may unite in yourfelf the admirable virtues of Genero-fity and Oeconomy, which will be the grace and crown of all your attainments, is the earneft wifh of

your ever affectionate.

H 3 LET-

L E T T E R   VIII.

WHILST you labour to enrich
your mind with the effential virtues of Chriftianity—with piety, benevolence, meeknefs, humility, integrity,
and purity—and to make yourfelf ufeful
in domeftic management, I would not
have my dear child neglect to perfue
thofe graces and acquirements, which
may fet her virtue in the moft advantageous light — adorn her manners — and
enlarge her underftanding : — and this,
not in the fpirit of vanity, but in the innocent and laudable view of rendering
herfelf more ufeful and pleafing to her fellow creatures, and confequently more
acceptable to God.—Politenefs of behaviour — and the attaining fuch branches

of

of knowledge, and such arts and accomplishments as are proper to your sex, capacity, and station—will prove so valuable to yourself through life, and will make you so desirable a companion, that the neglect of them may reasonably be deemed a neglect of duty—since it is undoubtedly our duty to cultivate the powers entrusted to us and to render ourselves as perfect as we can.

You must have often observed that nothing is so strong a recommendation on a slight acquaintance as *politeness*—nor does it lose its value by time or intimacy, when preserved, as it ought to be, in the nearest connections and strictest friendships. —This delightful qualification — so universally admired and respected, but so rarely possessed in any eminent degree— cannot but be a considerable object of my wishes for you :—nor should either of us be discouraged by the apprehension that neither I am capable of teaching, nor you of learning it, in *perfection* — since

H 4 whatever

whatever degree you attain will amply reward our pains.

To be perfectly polite, one muſt have great *preſence of mind*, with a delicate and quick *ſenſe of propriety* — or, in other words, one ſhould be able to form an inſtantaneous judgment of what is fitteſt to be ſaid or done, on every occaſion as it offers. — I have known one or two perſons, who ſeemed to owe this advantage to nature only, and to have the peculiar happineſs of being born, as it were, with another ſenſe, by which they had an immediate perception of what was proper and improper, in caſes abſolutely new to them :—But this is the lot of very few : —In general, propriety of behaviour muſt be the fruit of inſtruction, of obſervation and reaſoning ; and is to be cultivated and improved like any other branch of knowledge or virtue. — A good temper is a neceſſary ground-work of it ; and, if to this is added a good underſtanding, applied induſtriouſly to this purpoſe, I think it can hardly fail of attaining all that
is

is essential in it.—Particular modes and ceremonies of behaviour vary in different countries, and even in different parts of the same town. — These can only be learned by observation on the manners of those who are best skilled in them, and by keeping what is called good company. —But the principles of politeness are the same in all places.—Wherever there are human beings, it must be impolite to hurt the temper or to shock the passions of those you converse with.—It must every where be good-breeding, to set your companions in the most advantageous point of light, by giving each the opportunity of displaying their most agreeable talents, and by carefully avoiding all occasions of exposing their defects ; — to exert your own endeavours to please, and to amuse, but not to outshine them ; — to give each their due share of attention and notice — not engrossing the talk, when others are desirous to speak, nor suffering the conversation to flag, for want of introducing something to continue or renew a subject ;

H 5   —not

—not to puſh your advantages in argument ſo far that your antagoniſt cannot
retreat with honour : —— In ſhort, it is
an univerſal duty in ſociety to conſider
others more than yourſelf—— " in ho-
" nour preferring one another." ——
Chriſtianity, in this rule, gives the beſt
leſſon of politeneſs ; — yet judgement
muſt be uſed in the application of it :—
Our humility muſt not be ſtrained ſo far
as to diſtreſs thoſe we mean to honour ;—
we muſt not quit our proper rank, nor
force others to treat us improperly ; or to
accept, what we mean as an advantage,
againſt their wills. — We ſhould be perfectly eaſy, and make others ſo if we can.
— But, this happy eaſe belongs perhaps
to the laſt ſtage of perfection in politeneſs,
and can hardly be attained till we are con-
ſcious that we know the rules of behaviour,
and are not likely to offend againſt propriety. — In a very young perſon, who
has ſeen little or nothing of the world, this
cannot be expected ; but a real deſire of
obliging, and a reſpectful attention, will
in

in a great measure supply the want of
knowledge, and will make every one ready to overlook those deficiencies, which
are owing only to the want of opportunities to observe the manners of polite company. — You ought not therefore to be
too much depressed by the consciousness of
such deficiencies, but endeavour to get
above the shame of wanting what you
have not had the means of acquiring.—
Nothing heightens this false shame, and
the aukwardness it occasions, so much as
vanity — The humble mind, contented
to be known for what it is, and unembar-
rassed by the dread of betraying its ignorance, is present to itself, and can command the use of understanding, which
will generally preserve you from any great
indecorum, and will secure you from that
ridicule, which is the punishment of affectation rather than of ignorance.—People of sense will never despise you, whilst
you act naturally; but, the moment you
attempt to step out of your own character,
                                            you

you make yourself an object of juft ridicule.

Many are of opinion that a very young woman can hardly be too filent and re-ferved in company : —and certainly, no-thing is fo difgufting in youth as pertnefs and felf-conceit.—But, modefty fhould be diftinguifhed from an aukward bafhful-nefs, and filence fhould only be enjoined, when it would be forward and imperti-nent to talk.—There are many proper opportunities for a girl, young even as you are, to fpeak in company, with ad-vantage to herfelf—and, if fhe does it without conceit or affectation, fhe will al-ways be more pleafing than thofe, who fit like ftatues without fenfe or motion. — When you are filent, your looks fhould fhew your attention and prefence to the company : — a refpectful and earneft at-tention is the moft delicate kind of praife and never fails to gratify and pleafe.— You muft appear to be interefted in what is faid, and endeavour to improve your-felf by it :—if you underftand the fub-ject

ject well enough to aſk now and then a pertinent queſtion, or if you can mention any circumſtances relating to it that have not before been taken notice of, this will be an agreeable way of ſhewing your willingneſs to make a part of the company, and will probably draw a particular application to you, from ſome one or other. — Then, when called upon, you muſt not draw back as unwilling to anſwer, nor confine yourſelf merely to *yes* or *no*, as is the cuſtom of many young perſons, who become intolerable burthens to the miſtreſs of the houſe, whilſt ſhe ſtrives in vain to draw them into notice, and to give them ſome ſhare in the converſation.

In your father's houſe it is certainly proper for you to pay civility to the gueſts, and to talk to them in your turn—with modeſty and reſpect — if they encourage you to it. — Young ladies of near your own age, who viſit there, fall of courſe to your ſhare to entertain.—But, whilſt you exert yourſelf to make their viſit agreeable to them, you muſt not forget what is due to the elder part of the
company —

company—nor by whifpering and laughing apart, give them caufe to fufpect,
what is too often true, that they themfelves are the fubjects of your mirth.—
It is fo fhocking an outrage againft fociety to talk of, or laugh at any perfon in
his own prefence, that one would think it
could only be committed by the vulgar.—
I am forry however to fay, that I have
too often obferved it amongft young ladies, who little deferved that title whilft
they indulged their overflowing fpirits, in
defiance of decency and good-nature.—
The defire of laughing will make fuch in-
confiderate young perfons find a fubject
of ridicule, even in the moft refpectable
characters. — Old age, which — if not
difgraced by vice or affectation—has the
jufteft title to reverence, will be mimick-
ed and infulted ;—and even perfonal defects and infirmities will too often excite
contempt and abufe, inftead of compaffion. — If you have ever been led into
fuch an action, my dear girl, call it fe-
rioufly to mind, when you are confeffing
                                      your

your faults to Almighty God; and, be
fully perſuaded that it is not the leaſt
which you have to repent of.—You will
be immediately convinced of this, by
comparing it with the great rule of juſtice,
that of doing to all as you would they
ſhould do unto you —No perſon living is
inſenſible to the injury of contempt, nor
is there any talent ſo invidious, or ſo certain to create ill-will, as that of ridicule.
—The natural effects of years, which all
hope to attain, and the infirmities of the
body, which none can prevent, are ſurely
of all others the moſt improper objects of
mirth.—There are ſubjects enough that
are innocent, and on which you may freely indulge the vivacity of your ſpirits;—
for I would not condemn you to a perpetual ſeriouſneſs—on the contrary, I delight in a joyous temper, at all ages, and
particularly at yours.—Delicate and good-
natured raillery amongſt equal friends, if
pointed only againſt ſuch trifling errors as
the owner can heartily join to laugh at, or
ſuch qualities as they do not pique themſelves

felves upon, is both agreeable and ufeful;
but then it muft be offered in perfect kindnefs and fincere good humour; — if tinc-
tured with the leaft degree of malice, its
fting becomes venomous and deteftable.—
The perfon rallied fhould have liberty and
ability to return the jeft, which muft be
dropped upon the firft appearance of its
affecting the temper.

You will wonder perhaps, when I tell
you that there are fome characters in the
world, which I would freely allow you to
laugh at—though not in their prefence.
—Extravagant vanity, and affectation,
are the natural fubjects of ridicule, which
is their proper punifhment.— When you
fee old people, inftead of maintaining the
dignity of their years, ftruggling againft
nature to conceal them, affecting the
graces, and imitating the follies of youth.
— Or a young perfon affuming the importance and folemnity of old age—I do not
wifh you to be infenfible to the ridicule of
fuch abfurd deviations from truth and nature.—You are welcome to laugh, when
you

you leave the company, provided you lay
up a leſſon for yourſelf at the ſame time,
and remember, that unleſs you improve
your mind whilſt you are young, you alſo
will be an inſignificant fool in old age—
and that, if you are preſuming and arro-
gant in youth, you are as ridiculous as an
old woman with a head-dreſs of flowers.

In a young lady's behaviour towards
gentlemen, great delicacy is certainly required: yet, I believe, women oftener
err from too great a conſciouſneſs of the
ſuppoſed views of men than from inattention to thoſe views, or want of caution
againſt them.—You are at preſent rather
too young to want rules on this ſubject;—
but I could wiſh that you ſhould behave
almoſt in the ſame manner three years
hence as now;—and retain the ſimplicity
and innocence of childhood, with the
ſenſe and dignity of riper years.—Men
of looſe morals or impertinent behaviour
muſt always be avoided:—or if at any
time you are obliged to be in their company, you muſt keep them at a diſtance
by

by cold civility.—But, with regard to those gentlemen, whom your parents think it proper for you to converse with, and who give no offence by their own manners, to them I wish you to behave with the same franknefs and fimplicity as if they were of your own fex.—If you have natural modefty, you will never tranfgrefs its bounds, whilft you converfe with a man, as one rational creature with another, without any view to the poffibility of a lover or admirer, where nothing of that kind is profeft—where it is, I hope you will ever be equally a ftranger to coquetry and prudery—and that you will be able to diftinguifh the effects of real efteem and love from idle gallantry and unmeaning fine fpeeches: — the flighter notice you take of thefe laft, the the better; and that, rather with good-humoured contempt, than with affected gravity:—but the firft muft be treated with ferioufnefs and well-bred fincerity—not giving the leaft encouragement, which you do not mean—nor affuming airs of contempt,

contempt, where it is not deferved—
But this belongs to a fubject, which I have
touched upon in a former letter.—I have
already told you that you will be unfafe
in every ftep which leads to a ferious attachment, unlefs you confult your parents,
from the firft moment you apprehend any
thing of that fort is intended—let them
be your firft confidants, and let every part
of your conduct, in fuch a cafe, be particularly directed by them.

With regard to accomplifhments, the
chief of thefe is a competent fhare of
reading, well chofen and properly regulated ; and of this I fhall fpeak more largely
hereafter.—Dancing and the knowledge
of the French tongue are now fo univerfal, that they cannot be difpenfed with in
the education of a gentlewoman; and
indeed they both are ufeful as well as ornamental — the firft, by forming and
ftrengthening the body, and improving
the carriage ;—the fecond, by opening a
large field of entertainment and improvement for the mind.—I believe there are
more agreeable books of female literature
in

in French than in any other language—
and, as they are not lefs commonly talked
of than Englifh books, you muft often
feel mortified in company, if you are too
ignorant to read them.—Italian would
be eafily learnt after French — and, if
you have leifure and opportunity, may be
worth your gaining, though in your ftation of life it is by no means neceffary.

To write a free legible hand, and to underftand common arithmetic, are indifpen-
fable requifites.

As to mufic and drawing, I would only
wifh you to follow as Genius leads :— you
have fome turn for the firft, and I fhould
be forry to fee you neglect a talent, which
will at leaft afford you an innocent amufement, though it fhould not enable you to
give much pleafure to your friends :—I
think the ufe of both thefe arts is more
for yourfelf than for others :— it is but
feldom that a private perfon has leifure or
application enough to gain any high degree of excellence in them ;—and your
own partial family are perhaps the only
perfons who would not much rather be
entertained

entertained by the performance of a pro-
feffor than by yours : — but with regard to yourfelf it is of great confequence to have the power of filling up
agreeably thofe intervals of time, which
too often hang heavily on the hands of
a woman, if her lot be caft in a retired
fituation. — Befides this, it is certain,
that even a fmall fhare of knowledge in
thefe arts will heighten your pleafure in
the performances of others : — the tafte
muft be improved before it can be fufcep-
tible of an exquifite relifh for any of the
imitative arts : — An unfkilful ear is feldom capable of comprehending *Harmony*,
or of diftinguifhing the moft *delicate*
charms of *Melody*.—The pleafure of feeing fine paintings, or even of contem-
plating the beauties of Nature, muft be
greatly heightened by being converfant
with the rules of drawing, and by the
habit of confidering the moft picturefque
objects. — As I look upon tafte to be an
ineftimable fund of innocent delight, I
wifh you to lofe no opportunity of improving it, and of cultivating in yourfelf
the

the reliſh of ſuch pleaſures as will not interfere with a rational ſcheme of life, nor
lead you into diſſipation, with all its at-
tendant evils of vanity and luxury.

As to the learned languages, though I
reſpect the abilities and application of
thoſe ladies, who have attained them,
and who make a modeſt and proper uſe of
them, yet I would not adviſe you—or
any woman who is not ſtrongly impelled
by a particular genius—to engage in ſuch
ſtudies.—The labour and time which
they require are generally incompatible
with our natures and proper employments:
—the real knowledge which they ſupply
is not eſſential, ſince the Engliſh, French,
or Italian tongues afford tolerable tranſlations of all the moſt valuable productions
of antiquity, beſides the multitude of
original authors which they furniſh -and
theſe are much more than ſufficient to
ſtore your mind with as many ideas as you
will know how to manage.—The danger
of pedantry and preſumption in a woman,
of her exciting envy in one ſex and jea-
louſy

loufy in the other—of her exchanging the graces of imagination for the feverity and precifenefs of a fcholar, would be, I own, fufficient to frighten me from the ambition of feeing my girl remarkable for learning. —Such objections are perhaps ftill ftronger with regard to the abftrufe fciences.

Whatever tends to embellifh your fancy, to enlighten your underftanding, and furnifh you with ideas to reflect upon when alone, or to converfe upon in company, is certainly well worth your acquifition.— The wretched expedient, to which ignorance fo often drives our fex, of calling in flander to enliven the tedious infipidity of converfation, would alone be a ftrong reafon for enriching your mind with innocent fubjects of entertainment, which may render you a fit companion for perfons of fenfe and knowledge, from whom you may reap the moft defirable improvements:—for, though I think reading indifpenfably neceffary to the due cultivation of your mind, I prefer the converfation of fuch perfons to every other method
of

of inftruction: but, this you cannot hope
to enjoy unlefs you qualify yourfelf to
bear a part in fuch fociety, by, at leaft, a
moderate fhare of reading.

Though *religion* is the moft important of
all your perfuits, there are not many *books*
on that fubject, which I fhould recommend to you at prefent.—Controverfy is
wholly improper at your age, and it is
alfo too foon for you to enquire into the
evidence of the truth of revelation, or to
ftudy the difficult parts of fcripture:—
when thefe fhall come before you, there
are many excellent books, from which you
may receive great affiftance.—At prefent,
practical divinity—clear of fuperftition
and enthufiafm—but addreffed to the
heart, and written with a warmth and
fpirit capable of exciting in it pure and
rational piety, is what I wifh you to meet
with.

The principal ftudy I would recommend, is *hiftory*. — I know of nothing
equally proper to entertain and improve
at the fame time, or that is fo likely to
form

form and strengthen your judgment—and
by giving you a liberal and comprehensive
view of human nature, in some measure
to supply the defect of that experience,
which is usually attained too late to be of
much service to us:—Let me add, that
more materials for conversation are supplied by this kind of knowledge, than by
almost any other – but I have more to say
to you on this subject in a future letter.

The faculty, in which women usually
most excel, is that of imagination—and,
when properly cultivated, it becomes the
source of all that is most charming in society.—Nothing you can read will so
much contribute to the improvement of
this faculty as *poetry*—which, if applied
to its true ends, adds a thousand charms
to those sentiments of religion, virtue,
generosity, and delicate tenderness, by
which the human soul is exalted and
refined.—I hope you are not deficient
in natural taste for this enchanting art,
but that you will find it one of your
greatest pleasures to be conversant with

I   the

the beſt poets whom our language can bring you acquainted with, particularly, thoſe immortal ornaments of our nation, *Shakeſpear* and *Milton.*—The firſt is not only incomparably the nobleſt genius in dramatic poetry, but the greateſt maſter of nature, and the moſt perfect characteriſer of men and manners :—in this laſt point of view, I think him ineſtimable, and I am perſuaded that, in the courſe of your life, you will ſeldom find occaſion to correct thoſe obſervations on human nature, and thoſe principles of morality, which you may extract from his capital pieces.—You will at firſt find his language difficult; but if you take the aſſiſtance of a friend, who underſtands it well, you will by degrees enter into his manner of phraſeology, and perceive a thouſand beauties, which at firſt lay buried in obſolete words and uncouth conſtructions.—The admirable *Eſſay on Shakeſpear*, which has lately appeared, ſo much to the honour of our * ſex, will open your mind

* By Mrs. MONTAGUE;—and ſold at the Publiſhers of this Work.

mind to the peculiar excellencies of this author, and enlighten your judgment on dramatic poetry in general, with such force of reason and brilliancy of wit as cannot fail to delight as well as inftruct you.

Our great Englifh poet, Milton, is as far above my praife as his *Paradife Loft* is above any thing which I am able to read, except the Sacred Writers.—The fublimity of his fubject fometimes leads him into abftrufenefs—but many parts of his great poem are eafy to all comprehenfions, and muft find their way directly to every heart by the tendernefs and delicacy of his fentiments, in which he is not lefs ftrikingly excellent than in the richnefs and fublimity of his imagination. Addifon's criticifm in the Spectators, written with that beauty, elegance, and judgment, which diftinguifh all his writings, will aſſiſt you to underſtand, and to reliſh this poem.

It is needlefs to recommend to you the tranflations of Homer and Virgil, which every body reads that reads at all.—You

muft

muſt have heard that Homer is eſteemed the father of poetry—the original from whence all the moderns—not excepting Milton himſelf—borrow ſome of their greateſt beauties—and from whom they extract thoſe rules for compoſition, which are found moſt agreeable to nature, and true taſte.—Virgil, you know, is the next in rank amongſt the claſſics :—You will read his Æneid with extreme pleaſure, if ever you are able to read Italian, in Annibal Caro's tranſlation—the idiom of the Latin and Italian languages being more alike, it is I believe, much cloſer, yet preſerves more of the ſpirit of the original than the Engliſh tranſlations.

For the reſt, Fame will point out to you the moſt conſiderable of our poets—and I would not exclude any of name, among thoſe whoſe morality is unexceptionable : but of poets, as of all other authors, I wiſh you to read only ſuch as are properly recommended to you — ſince there are many who debaſe their divine art, by abuſing it to the purpoſes of vice and impiety.—

piety.—If you could read poetry with a judicious friend, who would lead your judgment to a true diſcernment of its beauties and defects, it would inexpreſſibly heighten both your pleaſure and improvement. But, before you enter upon this, ſome acquaintance with the *Heathen Mythology* is neceſſary. I think that you muſt before now have met with ſome book under the title of *The Pantheon :* — And, if once you know as much of the gods and goddeſſes as the moſt common books on the ſubject will tell you, the reſt may be learned by reading Homer . —but then you muſt particularly attend to him in this view.—I do not expect you to penetrate thoſe numerous myſteries--thoſe amazing depths of morality, religion, and metaphyſics — which ſome pretend to have diſcovered in his mythology ; - but, to know the names and principal offices of the gods and goddeſſes, with ſome idea of their moral meaning, ſeems requiſite to the underſtanding almoſt any poetical compoſition. — As an

I 3   inſtance

instance of the *moral meaning* I speak of, I
will mention an observation of Bossuet,
That Homer's poetry was particularly
recommended to the Greeks by the superiority which he ascribes to them over the
Asiatics — this superiority is shewn in the
Iliad, not only in the conquest of Asia by
the Greeks, and in the actual destruction
of its capital, but in the division and ar-
rangement of the Gods, who took part
with the contending nations.—On the
side of Asia was *Venus*—that is, sensual
passion—pleasure—and effeminacy. On
the side of Greece was *Juno*—that is,
matronly gravity and conjugal love; together with *Mercury* — invention and
eloquence — and *Jupiter* — or political
wisdom.—On the side of Asia was *Mars*,
who represents brutal valour and blind
fury.—On that of Greece was *Pallas*—
that is military discipline, and bravery,
guarded by judgment.

This, and many other instances that
might be produced, will shew you how
much of the beauty of the poet's art must
be

be loft to you, without fome notion of
thefe allegorical perfonages. — Boys, in
their fchool-learning have this kind of
knowledge impreffed on their minds by a
variety of books ; but women, who do
not go through the fame courfe of inftruction, are very apt to forget what little
they read or hear on the fubject: — I advife you therefore never to lofe an opportunity of enquiring the meaning of any
thing you meet with in poetry, or in painting, alluding to the hiftory of any of the
heathen deities, and of obtaining from
fome friend an explanation of its connection with true hiftory, or of its allegorical reference to morality or to phyfics.

Natural philofophy, in the largeft fenfe
of the expreffion, is too wide a field for
you to undertake — but the ftudy of nature, as far as may fuit your powers and
opportunities, you will find a moft fublime entertainment ; the objects of this
ftudy are all the ftupendous works of the
Almighty Hand that lie within the reach

I 4   of

of our obfervation. -- In the works of
man perfection is aimed at, but it can
only be found in thofe of the Creator.
The contemplation of perfection muft
produce delight — and every natural object around you would offer this delight,
if it could attract your attention :—if you
furvey the earth, every leaf that trembles
in the breeze — every blade of grafs beneath your feet is a wonder as abfolutely
beyond the reach of human art to imitate
as the conftruction of the univerfe. Endlefs pleafures, to thofe who have a tafte
for them, might be derived from the endlefs variety to be found in the compofition
of this globe and its inhabitants. The
foffil — the vegetable — and the animal
world — gradually rifing in the fcale of
excellence — the innumerable fpecies of
each, which preferve their fpecific diffe-
rences from age to age, yet of which no
two individuals are ever perfectly alike—
afford fuch a range for obfervation and
enquiry as might engrofs the whole term
of

of our short life, if followed minutely.—
Besides all the animal creation obvious to
our unassisted senses, the eye, aided by
philosophical inventions, sees myriads of
creatures, which by the ignorant are not
known to have existence: — it sees all
nature teem with life—every fluid—
each part of every vegetable and animal
swarm with its peculiar inhabitant, in-
visible to the naked eye, but as perfect in
all their parts, and enjoying life as indis
putably as the elephant or the whale.

But, if from the earth, and from these
minute wonders, the philosophic eye it
raised towards the Heavens, what a stus
pendous scene there opens to it's view!—
those brilliant lights that sparkle to the
eye of ignorance as gems adorning the
sky, or as lamps to guide the traveller,
assume an importance that amazes the
understanding ! —— they appear to be
worlds, formed like ours for a variety of
inhabitants — or *suns*, enlightening num
berless other worlds too distant for our

disco.

difcovery!—I fhall ever remember the
aftonifhment and rapture with which my
mind received this idea, when I was about
your age—it was then perfectly new to
me, and it is impoffible to defcribe the
fenfations, which I felt from the glorious,
boundlefs profpect of infinite beneficence
burfting at once upon my imagination!
—Who can contemplate fuch a fcene
unmoved?—if your curiofity is excited
to enter upon this noble enquiry, a few
books on the fubject, and thofe of the eafieft fort, with fome of the common ex-
periments, may be fufficient for your purpofe—which is to enlarge your mind,
and to excite in it the moft ardent gratitude and profound adoration towards that
great and good Being, who exerts his
boundlefs power in communicating vari-
our portions of happinefs through all the
immenfe regions of creation.

Moral philofophy—as it relates to human actions—is of ftill higher importance than the ftudy of nature.—The
works

works of the ancients on this subject are
univerfally faid to be entertaining as well
as inftructive, by thofe who can read them
in their original languages; — and fuch
of them as are well tranflated will undoubtedly, fome years hence, afford you
great pleafure and improvement. — You
will alfo find many agreeable and ufeful
books, written originally in French, and in
Englifh, on morals and manners : — for
the prefent, there are works, which,
without affuming the folemn air of philofophy, will enlighten your mind on thefe
fubjects, and introduce inftruction in an
eafier drefs :—of this fort are many of
the moral effays, which have appeared in
periodical papers — which, when excellent in their kind—as are the *Spectators*,
Guardians, *Ramblers*, and *Adventurers* —
are particularly ufeful to young people,
as they comprehend a great variety of fubjects — introduce many ideas and obfer-
vations that are new to them — and lead
to a habit of reflecting on the characters
and events that come before them in real
life,

life, which I confider as the beft exercife of the underftanding.

Books on tafte and criticifm will hereafter be more proper for you than at prefent: — whatever can improve your difcernment, and render your tafte elegant and juft, muft be of great confequence to your enjoyments as well as to the embellifhment of your underftanding.

I would by no means exclude the kind of reading, which young people are naturally moft fond of — though I think the greateft care fhould be taken in the choice of thofe *fictitious ftories*, that fo enchant the mind — moft of which tend to inflame the paffions of youth, whilft the chief purpofe of education fhould be to moderate and reftrain them. — Add to this, that both the writing and fentiments of moft novels and romances are fuch as are only proper to vitiate your ftile, and to miflead your heart and underftanding.—The expectation of extraordinary adventures — which feldom ever happen to the fober
                                    and

and prudent part of mankind—and the admiration of extravagant passions and abfurd conduct, are some of the usual fruits of this kind of reading — which, when a young woman makes it her chief amusement, generally renders her ridiculous in conversation, and miserably wrong-headed in her perfuits and behaviour.—There are however works of this class, in which excellent morality is joined with the most lively pictures of the human mind, and with all that can entertain the imagination and interest the heart.—But, I must repeatedly exhort you, never to read any thing of the sentimental kind, without taking the judgment of your best friends in the choice—for, I am perfuaded, that the indiscriminate reading of fuch kind of books corrupts more female hearts than any other cause whatsoever.

Before I close this correspondence, I shall point out the course of history I wish you to perfue, and give you my thoughts

of

of geography and chronology, some knowledge of both being, in my opinion, neceffary to the reading of hiftory with any
advantage.

I am, my deareft niece,

your ever affectionate.

L E T T E R IX.

MY DEAR NIECE,

I HAVE told you that you will not be able to read hiftory, with much plea- fure or advantage, without fome little knowledge of *Geography* and *Chronology.*— They are both very eafily attained — I mean in the degree that will be neceffary for you.—You muft be fenfible that you can know but little of a country, whofe fituation with refpect to the reft of the world you are entirely ignorant of—and that, it is to little purpofe that you are able to mention a fact, if you cannot nearly afcertain the *time* in which it hap- pened, which alone, in many cafes, gives importance to the fact itfelf.

In

In Geography—the eafieft of all fciences, and the beft adapted to the capacity of children—I fuppofe you to have made fome beginning:—to know at leaft the figure of the earth—the fuppofed lines— the degrees—how to meafure diftances —and a few of the common terms:—If you do not already know thefe, two or three leffons will be fufficient to attain them :—the reft is the work of memory, and is eafily gained by reading with maps;—for I do not wifh your knowledge to be exact and mafterly—but fuch only as is neceffary for the purpofe of underftanding hiftory, and, without which even a news-paper would be unintelligible.—It may be fufficient for this end, if, with refpect to *ancient* Geography, you have a general idea of the fituation of all the great ftates, without being able precifely to afcertain their limits.—But, in the *modern*, you ought to know the bounds and extent of every ftate in Europe, and its fituation with refpect to the reft,— The other parts of the world will require

less

lefs accurate knowledge, except with regard to the European fettlements.

It may be an ufeful and agreeable method, when you learn the fituation of any important country, to join with that knowledge fome one or two leading facts or circumftances concerning it, fo that its particular property may always put you in mind of the fituation, and the fituation, in like manner, recall the particular property.—When, for inftance, you learn in what part of the globe to find Ethiopia, to be told at the fame time that, in that vaft unknown tract of country, the Chriftian religion was once the religion of the ftate, would be of fervice—becaufe the geographical and hiftorical knowledge would affift each other.—Thus, to join with Egypt, *the nurfe and parent of arts and of fuperftition*—with Perfia, *fhocking defpotifm and perpetual revolutions*—with ancient Greece, *freedom and genius*—with Scythia, *hardinefs and conqueft*, are hints which you may make ufe of as you pleafe.—Perhaps annexing to any country the idea of fome

fome familiar form which it moſt refem-
bles, may at firſt aſſiſt you to retain a general notion of it—thus Italy has been
called a *boot*—and Europe compared to a
woman fitting.

The difference of the ancient and modern names of places is fomewhat perplexing—the moſt important ſhould be
known by both names at the fame time,
and you muſt endeavour to fix a few of
thofe which are of moſt confequence fo
ſtrongly in your mind, by thinking of
them, and being often told of them, that
the ancient name ſhall always call up the
modern one to your memory, and the
modern the ancient: — Such as the
Ægean fea, now *The Archipelago*—The
Peloponnefus, now *The Morea*—Crete,
Candia—Gaul, *France*—Babylon, *Bagdat*,
—Byzantium—to which the Romans
tranfplanted their feat of empire—*Con-
ſtantinople*, &c.

There have been fo many ingenious
contrivances to make geography eafy and
amufing, that I cannot hope to add any
thing

thing of much fervice;—I would only prevail with you not to neglect acquiring, by whatever method pleafes you beft, that fhare of knowledge in it, which you will find neceffary, and which is fo eafily attained—and I entreat that you would learn it in fuch a manner as to fix it in your mind, fo that it may not be loft and forgotten among other childifh acquifitions, but that it may remain ready for ufe through the reft of your life.

Chronology indeed has more of difficulty—but, if you do not bewilder yourfelf by attempting to learn too much and too minutely at firft, you need not defpair of gaining enough for the purpofe of reading hiftory with pleafure and utility.

Chronology may be naturally divided into three parts, *the Ancient—the Middle —and the Modern.*—With refpect to all thefe, the beft direction that can be given is to fix on fome periods or epochas, which, by being often mentioned and thought of, explained and referred to, will at laft be fo deeply engraven on the memory,

memory, that they will be ready to prefent themfelves whenever you call for them: —thefe indeed fhould be few, and ought to be well chofen for their importance, fince they are to ferve as elevated ftations to the mind, from which it may look backwards and forwards upon a great variety of facts.

Till your more learned friends fhall fupply you with better, I will take the liberty to recommend the following, which I have found of fervice to myfelf.

In the ancient chronology, you will find there were four thoufand years from the creation to the redemption of man—and that Noah and his family were miraculoufly preferved in the ark 1650 years after Adam's creation.

As there is no hiftory, except that in the Bible, of any thing before the flood, we may fet out from that great event, which happened, as I have faid above, in the year of the world 1650.

The

The 2350 years, which paffed from the deluge to our Saviour's birth, may be thus divided.—There have been four fuccef-five *Empires* called *Univerfal,* becaufe they extended over a great part of the then known world – thefe are ufually diftin-guifhed by the name of *The Four Great Monarchies* :— the three firft of them are included in ancient chronology, and begun and ended in the following man-ner :

1 ft, The Assyrian Empire, founded by Nimrod in the year of the world 1800, ended under Sardanapalus in 3250, en-dured 1450 years.

The Median—though not account-ed one of the four great monarchies, be-ing conquefts of rebels on the Affyrian empire—comes in here for about 200 years.

2d, The Persian Empire, which be-gan under Cyrus, in the year of the world 3450, ended in Darius in 3670, before Chrift 330, lafted a little more than 200 years.

3d, The

3d, The Grecian Empire, begun under Alexander the Great in 3670, was soon after his death difmembered by his fucceffors, but the different parcels into which they divided it were poffeffed by their refpective families, till the famous Cleopatra, the laft of the race of Ptolemy, one of Alexander's captains who reigned in Egypt, was conquered by Julius Cæfar, about half a century before our Lord's birth, which is a term of about 300 years.

Thus you fee that from the deluge to the eftablifhment of the firft great monarchy—the Affyrian—is—— 150 years.
The Affyrian empire conti-
    nued — — — — 1450
The Median — — — 200
The Perfian — — — 200
The Grecian — — — 300
From Julius Cæfar, with
    whom began the fourth
    great monarchy—viz. the
    Roman to Chrift — — —   50
                          ─────────
            In all — — 2350 years.
The term from the deluge to Chrift.

                                  If

If you confult books of Chronology, you will find errors of fome years in thefe dates — but exactnefs is not neceffary for a beginner—and I have taken only round numbers for the greater eafe of the memory.

I offer this fhort table as a little fpecimen of what you may eafily do for yourfelf - but even this fketch, flight as it is, will give you a general notion of the ancient hiftory of the world, from the deluge to the birth of Chrift.

Within this period flourifhed the Grecian and Roman republics, with the hiftory and chronology of which you will be required to be tolerably well acquainted ;— and indeed you will find nothing in the records of mankind fo entertaining.— Greece was divided into many petty ftates, whofe various revolutions and annals you can never hope diftinctly to remember— you are therefore to confider them as forming together one great kingdom— like the Germanic body, or the United Provinces—compofed feparately of different
rent

rent governments, but fometimes acting
with united force for their common intereft. — The *Lacedemonian* government,
formed by Lycurgus in the year of the
world 3100 - and the *Athenian*, regulated
by Solon about the year 3440 — will
chiefly engage your attention.

In purfuing the *Grecian* chronology, you
need only perhaps make one ftand or
epocha—at the time of *Socrates*, that wifeft
of philofophers, whom you muft have
heard of, who lived about 3570 years
from the creation, and about 430 before
Chrift — for within the term of 150 years
before Socrates, and 200 *after* him, will
fall in moft of the great events and illuftrious characters of the Grecian hiftory.

I muft inform you that the Grecian method of dating time was by *Olympiads*—
that is four compleat years—fo called
from the celebration, every fifth year, of
the Olympic Games, which were contefts
in all the manly exercifes, fuch as wreft-
ling—boxing—running- chariot-racing,
&c —They were inftituted in honour of
Jupiter,

Jupiter, and took their name from Olympia, a city of Elis, near which they were performed :—they were attended by all ranks of people, from every ftate in Greece ;—the nobleft youth were eager to obtain the prize of victory, which was no other than an olive crown, but efteemed the moft diftinguifhing ornament.— Thefe games continued all the time that Greece retained any fpark of liberty— and with them begins the authentic hiftory of that country—all before being confidered as fabulous.—You muft therefore endeavour to remember that they began in the year of the world 3228 — after the flood 1570 years — after the deftruction of Troy 400 — before the building of Rome 23—before Cyrus about 200 — and 770 before Chrift. If you cannot retain *all* thefe dates, at leaft you muft not fail to remember the coincidence of the *Olympiads* with the *building of Rome,* which is of great confequence, becaufe the Romans reckoned their time from the building of their city—indeed as thefe

K   two

two æras are within 23 years of each other, you may, for the eafe of memory, fuppofe them to begin together, in the year of the world 3228.

In reading the hiftory of the *Roman Republic*—which continued in that form of government to the time of Julius Cæfar's dictatorfhip, about the year of the world 3960, and about 48 years before Chrift—you will make as many epochas as you fhall find convenient:—I will mention only two—the facking of Rome by the Gauls, which happened in the year of the world 3620—in the 365th year of the city—in the 97th Olympiad —before Chrift 385—and about 30 years before the birth of Alexander.—The fecond epocha may be the 608th year of the city—when after three obftinate wars, Carthage was deftroyed, and Rome left without a rival.

Perhaps the following bad verfes, which were given me when I was young, may help to fix in your mind the important æras of the Roman and Grecian dates:—

You

You muſt not laugh at them, for chrono-
logers do not pique themſelves on their
poetry, but they make uſe of numbers
and rhymes merely as aſſiſtants to memory, being ſo eaſily learned by heart.

" Rome and Olympiads bear the ſame
 " date,
" Three thouſand two hundred and twen-
 " ty eight.
" In * three hundred and ſixty was Rome
 " ſack'd and torn,
" Thirty ſummers before Alexander was
 " born.

You will allow that what I have ſaid in
theſe few pages, is very eaſily learned —
yet little as it is, I will venture to ſay
that, were you as perfectly miſtreſs of it
as of your alphabet, you might anſwer
ſeveral queſtions relating to ancient chronology more readily, than many who pretend to know ſomething of this ſcience.—
One is not ſo much required to tell the
preciſe year, in which a great man lived,

K 2

as

* That is, in the 365th year of the city.

as to know with whom he was cotempo-
rary in other parts of the world. — I
would know then, from the flight fketch
above given, about what year of the Roman republic Alexander the Great lived.
—You would quickly run over in your
mind, " Alexander lived in the 3670th
" year of the world—330 before Chrift—
" confequently he muft have flourifhed
" about the *400th of Rome,* which had
" endured 750 years when Chrift was
" born."—In what condition was Greece,
at the time of the facking of Rome by
the Gauls — had any particular flate or
the united body, chofen then to take advantage of the misfortunes of the Romans? — You are to confider that the
365th year of the city—the date of that
event is 385 before Chrift—confequently
this muft have happened about the time
of Philip of Macedon, father of Alexander, when the Grecians, under fuch a
leader, might have extirpated the Roman
nation

nation from the earth, had they ever heard of them, or thought the conqueſt of them an object worthy their ambition.

Numberleſs queſtions might be anſwer'd in like manner, even on this very narrow circumſcribed plan, if it was completely maſtered. — I might require that other periods or epochas ſhould be learned with the ſame exactneſs but theſe may ſerve to explain my meaning, and to ſhew you how practicable and eaſy it is. One thing, however, I muſt obſerve—though perhaps it is ſufficiently obvious ——— which is—that you can make no uſe of this ſketch of ancient Chronology, nor even hope to retain it, till you have read the ancient *hiſtory.* — When you have gone through Rollin's Hiſtoire Ancienne *once,* then will be the time to fix the ancient Chronology deep in your mind, which will very much enhance the pleaſure and uſe of reading it a *ſecond* time—for you muſt remember, that nobody reads a hiſ-

tory

tory to much purpofe, who does not go over it more than once.

When you have got through your courfe of ancient hiftory, and are come to the more modern, you muft then have recourfe to the fecond of the three divifions — viz. *middle Chronology* — containing about 800 years, from the birth of our Lord, and from within 50 years of the rife of the Roman empire, to Charlemagne, who died in 814.

This period, except in the earlieft part of it, is too much involved in obfcurity to require a very minute knowledge of its hiftory — it may be fufficient to fix two or three of the moft fingular circumftances, by their proper dates.

The firft epocha to be obferved is the year of our Lord 330 — whenConftantine, the firft Chriftian emperor, who reftored peace to the oppreffed and perfecuted church, removed the feat of empire from Rome to Byzantium, called afterwards from

from him Conftantinople.—After his time — about the year 400 — began thofe irruptions of the Goths and Vandals, and other northern nations, who fettled themfelves all over the weftern parts of the Roman empire, and laid the foundation of the feveral ftates which now fubfift in Europe.

The next epocha is the year 622—for the eafe of memory, fay 600—when Mahomet, by his fuccefsful impofture, became the founder of the Saracen empire, which his followers extended over a great part of Afia and Africa, and over fome provinces of Europe.—At the fame time, St. Gregory, bifhop of Rome, began to affume a fpiritual power, which grew by degrees into that abfolute and enormous dominion, fo long maintained by the popes over the greateft part of Chriftendom.—St. Auguftine—a miffionary from St. Gregory—about this time, began the converfion of Great Britain to Chrifti anity.

The

The third and concluding epocha in this division is the year 800—when Charlemagne, king of France—after having subdued the Saxons, repreffed the Saracens, and eftablifhed the temporal dominion of the pope by a grant of confiderable territories – was elected emperor of the weft and protector of the church.— The date of this event correfponds with that remarkable period of our Englifh hiftory — the union of the Heptarchy — or feven kingdoms under Egbert.

As to the *third* part of chronology— namely the *Modern*, I fhall fpare you and myfelf all trouble about it at prefent, for, if you follow the courfe of reading which I fhall recommend, it will be fome years before you reach modern hiftory—and, when you do, you will eafily make periods for yourfelf, if you do but remember carefully to examine the dates as you read, and to imprefs on your memory thofe of very remarkable reigns or events.

I fear

I fear you are by this time tired of
Chronology—but, my fole intention in
what I have faid is to convince you that
it is a fcience not out of your reach, in the
moderate degree that is requifite for you:
—*the laſt volume of the Ancient Univerſal
Hiſtory* is the beſt Englifh Chronological
work I know—if that does not come in
your way, there is an excellent French
one called Tablettes Chronologiques de
l'Hiſtoire Univerfelle, Du Frefnoy, 3 vols.
Paris—there is alfo a *chart* of univerſal
hiſtory, including Chronology — and a
Biographical chart— both by Prieſtley—
which you may find of fervice to you.

Indeed, my dear, a woman makes a
poor figure who affects, as I have heard
fome ladies do, to difclaim all knowledge
of times and dates :—the ſtrange confufion they make of events, which happened in different periods, and the ſtare of
ignorance when fuch are referred to as
are commonly known, is fufficiently pi-
tiable:

K 5

tiable:—but the higheft mark of folly is to be proud of fuch ignorance—a refource in which fome of our fex find great confolation.

Adieu, my dear child—I am, with the tendereft affection,

ever yours.

L E T T E R X.

MY DEAR NIECE,

WHEN I recommend to you to gain some infight into the general hiftory of the world, perhaps you will think I propofe a formidable tafk—but, your apprehenfion will vanifh, when you confider that of near half the globe we have no hiftories at all;—that, of other parts of it, a few facts only are known to us—that, even of thofe nations, which make the greateft figure in hiftory, the early ages are involved in obfcurity and fable:—it is not indeed allowable to be totally ignorant even of thofe fables, be-caufe they are the frequent fubjects of

poetry

poetry and painting, and are often referred to in more authentic hiftories.

The firft recorders of actions are generally poets: — in the hiftorical fongs of
the bards are found the only accounts of
the firft ages of every ftate—but in thefe
we muft naturally expect to find truth
mixed with fiction, and often difguifed
in allegory.—In fuch early times, before
fcience has enlightened the minds of
men, the people are ready to believe every thing—and the hiftorian, having no
reftraints from the fear of contradiction or
criticifm, delivers the moft improbable
and abfurd tales as an account of the lives
and actions of their forefathers :—thus
the firft heroes of every nation are gods,
or the fons of gods—and every great
event is accompanied with fome fuperna-
tural agency, — Homer, whom I have
already mentioned as a poet, you will find
the moft agreeable hiftorian of the early
ages of Greece — and Virgil will fhew you
the

the fuppofed origin of the Carthaginians and Romans.

It will be neceffary for you to obferve fome regular plan in your hiftorical ftudies, which can never be perfued with advantage otherwife than in a continued feries.—I do not mean to confine you folely to that kind of reading—on the contrary, I wifh you frequently to relax with poetry or fome other amufement, whilft you are perfuing your courfe of hiftory ; I only mean to warn you againft mixing *ancient* hiftory with *modern*, or *general* hiftories of one place with *particular reigns* in another—by which defultory manner of reading, many people diftract and confound their memories, and retain nothing to any purpofe from fuch a confufed mafs of materials.

The moft ancient of all hiftories, you will read in your Bible—thence you will proceed to L' Hiftoire Ancienne of Rollin, who very ingenioufly points out the connection of profane with facred hiftory,

tory, and enlivens his narrative with
many agreeable and improving reflections
—and many very pleasing detached sto-
ries and anecdotes, which may serve you
as resting places in your journey.—It
would be an useful exercise of your memory and judgment, to recount these interesting passages to a friend, either by
letter or in conversation—not in the
words of the author, but in your own natural stile—by memory and not by book
and to add whatever remarks may occur
to you. — I need not say that you will
please me much, whenever you are dif-
posed to make this use of *me*.

The want of memory is a great discou-
ragement in historical persuits, and is
what every body complains of.—Many
artificial helps have been invented, of
which, those who have tried them can
best tell you the effects: — but the most
natural and pleasant expedient is that of
conversation with a friend, who is acquainted with the history which you are
reading.

reading. — By fuch converfations, you will find out how much is ufually retained of what is read, and you will learn to felect thofe characters and facts which are beft worth preferving : — for, it is by trying to remember every thing without diftinction, that young people are fo apt to lofe every trace of what they read.—By repeating to your friend what you can recollect, you will fix it in your memory ; and, if you fhould omit any ftriking particular, which ought to be retained, that friend will remind you of it, and will direct your attention to it on a fecond perufal.—It is a good rule, to caft your eye each day over what you read the day before, and to look over the contents of every book when you have finifhed it.

Rollin's work takes in a large compafs —but, of all the ancient nations it treats of, perhaps there are only the Grecian and Roman, whofe ftories ought to be read with any anxious defire of retaining
them

them perfectly :—for the reſt—ſuch as
the Aſſyrians, Egyptians, &c. — I believe, you will find, on examination,
that moſt of thoſe who are ſuppoſed tolerably well read in hiſtory, remember no
more than a few of the moſt remarkable
facts and characters.—I tell you this to
prevent your being diſcouraged on finding
ſo little remain in your mind after reading
theſe leſs intereſting parts of ancient hiſtory.

But, when you come to the Grecian
and Roman ſtories, I expect to find you
deeply intereſted and highly entertained ;
—and, of conſequence, eager to treaſure
up in your memory thoſe heroic actions
and exalted characters, by which a young
mind is naturally ſo much animated and
impreſſed. —— As Greece and Rome
were diſtinguiſhed as much for genius as
valour, and were the theatres, not only
of the greateſt military actions — the
nobleſt efforts of liberty and patriotiſm—
but of the higheſt perfection of arts and
                              ſciences,

fciences, their immortal fame is a fubject
of wonder and emulation, even to thofe
diftant ages ; — and, it is thought a
fhameful degree of ignorance, even in our
fex, to be unacquainted with the nature
and revolutions of their governments,
and with the characters and ftories of
their moft illuftrious heroes.—Perhaps,
when you are told that the government
and the national character of your own
countrymen have been compared with
thofe of the Romans, it may not be an
ufelefs amufement, when you read the
Roman Hiftory, to carry this obfervation
in your mind, and to examine how far the
parallel holds good.—The French have
been thought to refemble the Athenians
in their genius, though not in their love
of liberty.—Thefe little hints fometimes
ferve to awaken reflection and attention
in young readers — I leave you to make
what ufe of them you pleafe.

When you have got through Rollin, if
you add *Vertot's Rovolutions Romaines* — a
fhort,

fhort, and very entertaining work—you may be faid to have read as much as is *abfolutely neceffary* of ancient hiftory.—Plutarch's Lives of famous Greeks and Romans—a book defervedly of the higheft reputation — can never be read to fo much advantage as immediately after the hiftories of Greece and Rome :—I fhould even prefer reading each life in Plutarch, immediately after the hiftory of each particular Hero, as you meet with them in Rollin or in Vertot.

If hereafter you fhould choofe to enlarge your plan, and fhould wifh to know more of any particular people or period than you find in Rollin, the fources from which he drew may be open to you — for there are, I believe, French or Englifh tranflations of all the original hiftorians from whom he extracted his materials.

Crevier's continuation of Rollin, I believe, gives the beft account of the Roman emperors down to Conftantine.—
What

What shocking instances will you there
meet with, of the terrible effects of law-
less power on the human mind!—How
will you be amazed to see the most pro-
mising characters changed by flattery and
self-indulgence into monsters that disgrace
humanity!—to read a series of such lives
as those of Tiberius, Nero, or Domitian,
would be intolerable, were we not consol-
ed by the view of those excellent emperors, who remained uncorrupted through
all temptations.—When the mind—dif-
gusted, depressed, and terrified—turns
from the contemplation of those depths
of vice, to which the human nature may
be sunk, a Titus, the delight of mankind
—a Trajan—an Antoninus — restore it
to an exulting sense of the dignity, to
which that nature may be exalted by virtue. — Nothing is more awful than this
consideration :— a human creature given
up to vice is infinitely below the most abject brute — the same creature, trained
by virtue to the utmost perfection of his
nature,

nature, " is but a little lower than the
" angels, and is crowned with glory and
" immortality."

Before you enter upon the modern hiftory of any particular kingdom, it will be
proper to gain fome idea of that interval
between ancient and modern times, which
is juftly called the dark and barbarous
ages — and which lafted from Conftantine to Charlemagne — perhaps one might
fay to fome centuries after. — On the ir-
ruption of the northern Barbarians, who
broke the Roman empire, and diffipated
all the treafures of knowledge, as well as
of riches, which had been fo long accumu-
lating in that enormous ftate, the European world may be faid to have returned
to a fecond infancy ; — and the Monkifh
legends, which are the only records preferved of the times in which they were
written, are no lefs fabulous than the tales
of the demi-gods.—I muft profefs myfelf
ignorant how to direct you to any diftinct
or amufing knowledge of the hiftory of
Europe

Europe during this period : — ſome col-
lect it from *Puffendorf's Introduction* —
ſome from *The Univerſal Hiſtory* — and
now, perhaps, with more advantage and
delight, from the firſt volume of *Robertſon's Charles the Fifth,* in which he traces
the progreſs of civilization, government,
and arts, from the firſt ſettlements of the
Barbarians ; and ſhews the foundation of
the ſeveral ſtates, into which Europe is
now divided, and of theſe laws, cuſtoms,
and politics, which prevail in this quarter
of the world.

In theſe dark ages, you will find no
ſingle character ſo intereſting as that of
Mahomet—that bold impoſtor, who extended his uſurped dominion equally over
the minds and properties of men, and
propagated a new religion, whilſt he
founded a new empire, over a large portion of the globe.—His life has been
written by various hands.

When you come to the particular hiſtories of the European ſtates, your own
country,

country ſeems to demand the precedence
—and, there is no part more commodious to ſet out from, ſince you cannot
learn the hiſtory of Great Britain, without
becoming in ſome degree acquainted with
almoſt every neighbouring nation, and
without finding your curioſity excited to
know more of thoſe, with whom we are
moſt connected.

By the amazing progreſs of navigation
and commerce, within the laſt two or
three centuries, all parts of the world are
now connected : — the moſt diſtant people are become well acquainted, who, for
thouſands of years, never heard of one
another's exiſtence : — we are ſtill every
day exploring new regions — and every
day ſee greater reaſon to expect that immenſe countries may yet be diſcovered,
and America no longer retain the name of
the *New World*. — You may paſs to every quarter of the earth, and find yourſelf ſtill in the Britiſh dominion ; — this
iſland, in which we live, is the leaſt portion

tion of it — and if we were to adopt the
ſtile of the ancient conquerors, we might
call it the throne, from which we rule the
world. — To this boaſt we are better en-
titled than ſome of thoſe who formerly
called themſelves *Maſters of the Globe*, as
we poſſeſs an empire of greater extent,
and, from the ſuperior advantages of our
commerce, much greater power and
riches; — but, we have now too many
rivals in dominion to take upon us ſuch
haughty titles.

You cannot be ſaid to know the hiſtory
of that empire, of which you are a ſubject, without knowing ſomething of the
Eaſt and Weſt Indies, where ſo great a
part of it is ſituated;—and you will find
the accounts of the diſcovery and conqueſt of America very entertaining, tho'
you will be ſhocked at the injuſtice and
cruelty of its conquerors. — But, with
which of the glorious conquerors of mankind muſt not humanity be ſhocked! —
Ambition, the moſt remorſeleſs of all paſſions, perſues it object by all ſorts of
means:—

means :—juſtice, mercy, truth, and every
thing moſt ſacred, in vain oppoſe its progreſs! — alas, my dear, ſhall I venture
to tell you that the hiſtory of the world is
little elſe than a ſhocking account of the
wickedneſs and folly of the ambitious !—
The world has ever been, and, I ſuppoſe,
ever muſt be, governed and inſulted by
theſe aſpiring ſpirits — has always, in a
greater or leſs degree, groaned under their
unjuſt uſurpation.

But let not the horror of ſuch a ſcene
put a ſtop to your curioſity—it is proper
you ſhould know mankind as they are.—
You muſt be acquainted with the heroes
of the earth, and perhaps you may be
too well reconciled to them :—Mankind
have in general a ſtrong bias in their favour; — we ſee them ſurrounded with
pomp and ſplendour — every thing that
relates to them has an air of grandeur—
and, whilſt we admire their natural powers, we are too apt to pardon the deteſta-
ble abuſe of them, to the injury and ruin
of the human race.—We are dazzled with
                                        falſe

falfe glory, and willingly give into the delufion; for mighty conquefts, like great conflagrations, have fomething of the fublime that pleafes the imagination, tho' we know, if we reflect at all, that the confequences of them are devaftation and mifery.

The Weftern and Eaftern world will prefent to you very different profpects.— In *America*, the firft European conquerors found nature in great fimplicity—fociety ftill in its infancy—and confequently the arts and fciences yet unknown :—fo that the facility, with which they overpowered thefe poor innocent people, was entirely owing to their fuperior knowledge in the arts of deftroying.—They found the inhabitants brave enthufiaftic patriots, but without either the military or political arts neceffary for their defence. — The two great kingdoms of Mexico and Peru had alone made fome progrefs in civilization— they were both formed into regular ftates, and had gained fome order and difcipline : —from thefe therefore the Spaniards met with fomething like an oppofition.— At firft indeed the invaders appeared fuper-

L   natural

natural beings, who came upon them flying over the ocean, on the wings of the wind, and who, mounted on fiery animals, unknown in that country, attacked them with thunder and lightning in their hands—for such the fire-arms of the Spaniards appeared to this aftonifhed people.—But, from being worfhipped as gods, they foon came to be feared as evil fpirits;—and in time being difcovered to be men—different from the Americans only in their outrageous injuftice, and in the cruel arts of deftroying,—they were abhorred and boldly oppofed.—The refiftance however of a million of thefe poor naked people, defperately crouding on each other to deftruction, ferved only to make their ruin more complete.—The Europeans have deftroyed, with the moft fhocking barbarity, many millions of the original inhabitants of thefe countries, and have ever fince been depopulating Europe and Africa to fupply their places.

Though our own countrymen have no reafon to boaft of the juftice and humanity of their proceedings in America, yet, in comparifom with thofe of the Spaniards,

our

our poſſeſſions there were innocently acquired.—Some of them were gained by
conqueſt or ceſſion, from Spain and from
other European powers.—Some by contract with the natives, or by ſettlements
on uninhabited lands.—We are now poſ-
ſeſſed of a ſeries of colonies, extending
above two thouſand miles along the whole
Eaſtern coaſt of North America, beſides
many iſlands of immenſe value.—Theſe
countries, inſtead of being thinly peopled
by a few herds of ignorant ſavages, are
now adorned with many great cities, and
innumerable rich plantations, which have
made ample returns to their mother country, for the dangers and expences which
attended their firſt eſtabliſhment.—Bleſt
with more natural advantages than almoſt
any country in the world, they are making
a ſwift progreſs in wealth and grandeur,
and ſeem likely, in ſome future period, to
be as much the ſeat of empire and of ſcience as Europe is at preſent.—Whether
their attainments in virtue and happineſs
will keep pace with their advancement in
knowledge, wealth, and power, is much
to be queſtioned—for you will obſerve, in
your hiſtorical view of the ſeveral great

empires

empires of the world, that as each grew up towards the higheſt pitch of greatneſs, the ſeeds of deſtruction grew up with it : — Luxury and vice, by debaſing the minds, and enervating the bodies of the people, left them all, in their turns, an eaſy prey to poorer and more valiant nations.

In the Eaſt, the Europeans introduced themſelves in a milder way :—admitted firſt as traders—and, for the more commodious carrying on their commerce, indulged by the powers of the country, in eſtabliſhing a few ſmall factories—they by gentle degrees extended and ſtrengthened their ſettlements there, till their force became conſiderable enough to be thought an uſeful auxiliary to contending princes ;—and — as it has often happened to thoſe who have called in foreign powers to interfere in their domeſtic contentions by availing themſelves of the diſturbances of a diſmembered monarchy, they at length raiſed a power, almoſt independent of their employers. Soon, the ſeveral European nations, who had thus got footing in the Indies, jealous of each other's growing greatneſs, made the feuds

of

of the native princes fubfervient to their
mutual contefts—till within a few years,
the Englifh, by a happy concurrence of
circumftances, obtained the maftery, and
expelled their rivals from all their confiderable fettlements.

The rapidity of our conquefts here has
equalled nearly that of the firft invaders
of America—but from different caufes. —
Here we found an old eftablifhed empire
advanced to its crifis—the magnificence
and luxury of the great carried to the
higheft excefs, and the people in a propor-
tionable degree of oppreffion and debafe-
ment.—Thus ripe for deftruction, the ri-
valfhips of the viceroys, from the weaknefs of the government, became independent fovereigns — and the daftardly
fpirit of the meaner people, indifferent to
the caufe for which they were compelled
to fight—encouraged thefe ambitious mer-
chants to pufh their advantages farther
than they could at firft have fuppofed poffible:—with aftonifhment they faw the
intrepid leaders of a few hundreds of brave
free Britons boldly oppofe and repeatedly
put to flight millions of thefe effeminate

L 3 Indian

Indian flaves—and, in a fhort time, raife from them an empire much larger than their Mother Country.

From thefe remote quarters of the world, let us now return to Great Britain, with the hiftory of which, you ought certainly to acquaint yourfelf, before you enter upon that of any other European kingdom.—If you have courage and induftry enough to begin fo high as the invafion of Julius Cæfar—before which nothing is known of the inhabitants of this ifland—you may fet out with Rapin, and proceed with him to William the Conqueror—From this æra there are other hiftories of England more entertaining than his, though, I believe, none efteemed more authentic.—Party fo ftrongly influences both hiftorians and their readers, that it is a difficult and invidious tafk to point out the *beft* amongft the number of Englifh hiftories that offer themfelves :— but as *you* will not read with a critical view, nor enter deeply into politics, I think you may be allowed to choofe that which is moft entertaining—and, in this view, I believe the general voice will direct to Hume, though he goes no farther than

than the Revolution.—Among other *hifto-rians*, do not forget my darling *Shakefpear* —a faithful as well as a moft agreeable one—whofe hiftorical plays, if read in a feries, will fix in your memory the reigns he has chofen, more durably than any other hiftory.—You need not fear his leading you into any material miftakes, for he keeps furprizingly clofe to the truth as well in the characters as in the events. —One cannot but wifh he had given us a play on the reign of every Englifh king —as it would have been the pleafanteft, and perhaps the moft ufeful way of be-coming acquainted with it.

For the other portion of Great Britain, Robertfon's hiftory of Scotland is a de-lightful work, and of a moderate fize.

Next to your own country, *France* will be the moft interefting object of your en-quiries—our ancient fettlements in that country, and the frequent contefts we have been engaged in with its inhabitants, connect their hiftory with our own. —The extent of their dominion and influence — their fuppofed fuperiority in elegance and politenefs — their eminence in the Arts

and

and Sciences – and that intercourſe of thought—if I may ſo call it—which ſub-ſiſts between us, by the mutual communication of literary productions — make them peculiarly intereſting to us ;—and we cannot but find our curioſity excited to know their ſtory, and to be intimately acquainted with the character, genius, and ſentiments of this nation.

I do not know of any general hiſtory of France that will anſwer your purpoſe except that of *Mezerai;* which, even in the abridgement is a pretty large work — there is a very modern one by *Velly,* *and others,* which perhaps may be more lively, but is ſtill more voluminous, and not yet compleated.—From Mezerai, you may proceed with Voltaire to the end of Louis the Fourteenth.

In conſidering the reſt of Europe, your curioſity may be confined within narrower limits.—Modern hiſtory is, from the nature of it, much more minute and laborious than the ancient — and to perſue that of ſo many various kingdoms and governments would be a taſk unequal to your leiſure and abilities, at leaſt for ſeveral

veral years to come;—at the fame time,
it muſt be owned, that the preſent ſyſtem
of politics and commerce has formed ſuch
a relation between the different powers of
Europe, that they are in a manner mem-
bers of one great body—and a total ignorance of any conſiderable ſtate would
throw an obſcurity even upon the affair
of your own country :—an acquaintance
however with the moſt remarkable circumſtances that diſtinguiſh the principal
governments, will ſufficiently enlighten
you, and will enable you to comprehend,
whatever relates to them, in the hiſtories
which you are more familiar with. — Inſtead of referring you for this purpoſe to
dull and unintereſting abridgments, I
chooſe rather to point out to you a few
ſmall Tracts, which exhibit ſtriking and
lively pictures, not eaſily effaced from the
memory, of the conſtitutions and the
moſt remarkable tranſactions of ſeveral
of theſe nations. — Such are

Sir William Temple's Eſſay on the United Provinces.

His Eſſay on Heroic Virtue, which contains ſome Account of the Saracen
Empire.

Vertot's

Vertot's Revolutions de Suede.
———— ———— ——— de Portugal.
Voltaire's Charles XII. de Suede.
———— —— Pierre le Grand.
Puffendorf's Account of the Popes, in his
    Introduction to Modern Hiſtory.

Some part of the Hiſtory of Germany
and Spain, you will ſee more in detail in
Robertſon's Hiſtory of Charles the Vth,
which I have already recommended to you
in another view.

After all this, you may ſtill be at a loſs
for the tranſactions of Europe in the laſt
fifty years – for the purpoſe of giving you,
in a very ſmall compaſs, ſome idea of the
ſtate of affairs during that period, I will
venture to recommend one book more—
Campbell's State of Europe.

Thus much may ſuffice for that moderate ſcheme, which I think is beſt ſuited
to your ſex and age.—There are ſeveral
excellent hiſtories, and memoirs of particular reigns and periods, which I have
taken no notice of in this circumſcribed
plan—but, with which, if you ſhould
happen to have a taſte for the ſtudy, you
will hereafter chooſe to be acquainted :—
                theſe

theſe will be read with moſt advantage, after you have gained ſome general view of hiſtory—and they will then ſerve to refreſh your memory, and ſettle your ideas diſtinctly, as well as enable you to compare different accounts of the perſons and facts which they treat of, and to form your opinions of them on juſt grounds.

As I cannot, with certainty, foreſee what degree of application or genius for ſuch perſuits you will be miſtreſs of, I ſhall leave the deficiencies of this collection to be ſupplied by the ſuggeſtions of your more informed friends—who, if you explain to them how far you wiſh to extend your knowledge, will direct you to the proper books.

But if, inſtead of an eager deſire for this kind of knowledge, you ſhould happen to feel that diſtaſte for it which is too common in young ladies, who have been indulged in reading only works of mere amuſement, you will perhaps rather think that I want mercy in offering you ſo large a plan, than that there needs an apology for the deficiencies of it:—but, comfort yourſelf with the aſſurance that a taſte for hiſtory hiftory will grow and improve by reading —that as you get acquainted with one period or nation, your curiofity cannot fail to be awakened for what concerns thofe immediately connected with it—and thus, you will infenfibly be led on, from one degree of knowledge to another.

If you wafte in trivial amufement the next three or four years of your life, which are the prime feafon of improvement, believe me, you will hereafter bitterly regret their lofs:—when you come to feel yourfelf inferior in knowledge to almoft every one you converfe with—and, above all, if you fhould ever be a mother, when you feel your own inability to direct and affift the perfuits of your children:—you will then find ignorance a fevere mortification, and a real evil.— Let this, my dear, animate your induftry —and let not a modeft opinion of your own capacity be a difcouragement to your endeavours after knowledge—a moderate underftanding, with diligent and well-directed application, will go much farther than a more lively genius, if attended with that impatience and inattention, which

too

too often accompany quick parts—It is not for want of capacity that ſo many women are ſuch trifling, inſipid companions—ſo ill qualified for the friendſhip and converſation of a ſenſible man—or for the taſk of governing and inſtructing a family ; — it is much oftener from the neglect of exerciſing the talents, which they really have, and from omitting to cultivate a taſte for intellectual improvement : — by this neglect they loſe the ſincereſt of pleaſures — a pleaſure, which would remain when almoſt every other forſakes them — which neither fortune nor age can deprive them of—and which would be a comfort and reſource in almoſt every poſſible ſituation of life.

If I can but inſpire you, my dear child, with the deſire of making the moſt of your time and abilities, my end is anſwered — the means of knowledge will eaſily be found by thoſe who diligently ſeek them —and they will find their labours, abundantly rewarded.

And now, my dear, I think it is time to finiſh this long correſpondence — which, though in ſome parts it may have
been

been tedious to you, will not, I hope, be found entirely ufelefs in any. — I have laid before you all that my matureft reflections could enable me to fuggeft, for the direction of your conduct through life. — My love for you, my deareft child, extends its views beyond this frail and tranfitory exiftence—it confiders you as a candidate for immortality—as entering the lifts for the prize of your high calling — as contending for a crown of unfading glory.—It fees, with anxious folicitude, the dangers that furround you, and the everlafting fhame that muft follow, if you do not exert all your ftrength in the conflict. — Religion therefore has been the bafis of my plan—the principle, to which every other perfuit is ultimately referred. —Here then I have endeavoured to guide your refearches, and to affift you in forming juft notions on a fubject of fuch infinite importance.—I have fhewn you the neceffity of regulating your heart and temper, according to the genuine fpirit of that religion, which I have fo earneftly recommended as the great rule of your
life.

life. — To the fame principle, I would
refer your attention to domeftic duties—
and, even that refinement and elegance
of manners, and all thofe graces and accomplifhments which will fet your virtues in the faireft light, and will engage
the affection and refpect of all who converfe with you. — Endeared to Society
by thefe amiable qualities, your influence
in it will be more extenfive, and your capacity of being ufeful proportionably enlarged. — The ftudies, which I have recommended to you, muft be likewife
fubfervient to the fame views;—the perfuit of knowledge, when it is guided and
controul'd by the principles I have eftablifh'd, will conduce to many valuable
ends :—the habit of induftry, it will give
you — the nobler kind of friendfhips,
for which it will qualify you. and its ten-
dency to promote a candid and liberal way
of thinking, are obvious advantages. I
might add, that a mind well informed in
the various perfuits which intereft mankind, and the influence of fuch perfuits
on their happinefs, will embrace, with a
clearer

clearer choice, and will more fteadily adhere to, thofe principles of Virtue, and Religion, which the judgment muft ever approve in proportion as it becomes enlighten'd.

May thofe delightful hopes be anfwer'd which have animated my heart, while with diligent attention I have endeavour'd to apply to your advantage all that my own experience and beft obfervation could furnifh.—With what joy fhould I fee my deareft girl fhine forth a bright example of every thing that is amiable and praifeworthy!—and how fweet would be the reflection that I had, in any degree, contributed to make her fo!—My heart expands with the affecting thought, and pours forth in this adieu the moft ardent wifhes for your perfection!—If the tender folicitude exprefs'd for your welfare by this " labour of love" can engage your gratitude, you will always remember how deeply your conduct interefts the happinefs of

Your moft affectionate Aunt.

T H E   E N D.

For EU product safety concerns, contact us at Calle de José Abascal, 56–1°, 28003 Madrid, Spain or eugpsr@cambridge.org.

www.ingramcontent.com/pod-product-compliance
Ingram Content Group UK Ltd.
Pitfield, Milton Keynes, MK11 3LW, UK
UKHW010343140625
459647UK00010B/783